First-Line Supervision

Fifth Edition

First-Line Supervision

Fifth Edition

Charles M. Cadwell

AMA American Management Association®

First-Line Supervision, Fith Edition

© 2006, 1999 American Management Association International. All rights reserved. This material may not be reproduced, stored in a retrieval system, or transmitted in whole or in part, in any form or by any means, electronic, mechanical, photocopying, recording, or otherwise, without the prior written permission of the publisher.

ISBN: 978-0-7612-1451-9

AMACOM Self-Study Program
http://www.amaselfstudy.org

AMERICAN MANAGEMENT ASSOCIATION
http://www.amanet.org

Printing number
16   17   18   19   20   21

Contents

About This Course — xi
How to Take This Course — xiii
Pre-Test — xv

1 Becoming a Supervisor — 1

Making the Transition to First-Line Supervisor
   Focus
   Seeing the Big Picture
   The Work
   Number of Priorities
   Work Quality
   Time Commitment
   Dealing with Information
   Motivation
   Role on the Team
   Attitude

Importance of First-Line Supervision
   Day-to-Day Operations
   First Line of Contact for Employees
   Span of Control
   Development of Organization Talent

Paradoxes of First-Line Supervision
   Being a Supervisor and a Technical Expert
   Little Effort Is Devoted to Training
   The Way Work Is Organized
   Supervising Tasks and Learning Skills

Leadership Style and Behavior
   Task vs. People
   Other Considerations Affecting Leadership Style

Recap
Review Questions

2 Role of the Supervisor   21

Day-to-Day Supervisory Roles
- Plan and Organize Work
- Provide Resources
- Manage and Develop People
- Administer and Control
- Handle Problems and Issues

Personal Qualities of an Effective First-Line Supervisor
- Set High Personal Standards
- Be Accessible
- Inspire Success
- Accept Responsibility for Your Actions
- Emphasize Quality and Service
- Believe in Employees
- Set Priorities and Stick to Them
- Strive for Continuous Improvement

Working with Your Boss
- Develop a Partnership
- Focus on Common Priorities
- Communicate Upward
- Maximize the Relationship Potential

First-Line Supervision Key Competencies
- Communicating
- Developing People
- Managing People
- Building a Team
- Getting the Work Done
- Supervising in a Changing Environment

Recap
Review Questions

3 Communicating   45

The Communication Process

Listener Problems and Solutions
- What Is This All About?
- Exactly What Is Being Proposed?
- Why Is It Needed and by Whom?
- What's in It for Me?
- What Is Supposed to Be Done About It?

Improving Personal Listening Habits
- Listen for Ideas, Emotions, and Feelings
- Listen for What Is Not Being Said
- Control Your Emotional Reactions
- Overcome Personal Prejudgments and Distractions
- Keep an Open Mind
- Listen More Than You Talk
- Hear the Other Person Out (Don't Interrupt)
- Use Open-Ended Questions for Active Listening

Planning and Conducting Meetings
  Preparing an Agenda
  Conducting the Meeting
  After the Meeting
  Brainstorming
Written Communication
  Organize Before You Write
  Use Simple, Straightforward Language
  Be Sensitive to the Tone of Your Writing
  Write from the Viewpoint of the Reader
Communication Technology
  Electronic Messaging
  Voice Mail
  Internet or Intranet
  Conferencing
  Cellular Technology
  Computer Systems
Recap
Review Questions

4 Developing People — 71
People Development
  Benefits
  Types of Development Activities
  Setting Goals and Maintaining Focus
New Employee Orientation
  Objectives
  Developing an Orientation Plan
  Conducting New Employee Orientation
Employee Training
  Benefits of Training
  Failure to Train
  Identifying Training Needs
  Four-Step Training Method
  Being an Effective Trainer
Making Sure Training Is Effective
  Have a Pre-Training Meeting
  Have a Post-Training Meeting
  Provide an Opportunity to Perform
  Ensure a Supportive Environment
  Encourage and Recognize Improvements
Coaching Employees
  Key Factors in Assessing a Possible Coaching Situation
  The Coaching Process
  When to Quit Coaching
Recap
Review Questions

5　Managing People　　99

Performance Feedback
- Using Feedback Systems
- Provide Positive Feedback to Reinforce Performance
- Providing Corrective Feedback
- Performance Appraisal as a Feedback Tool

Working with Difficult Employees
- Types of Difficult Behaviors
- Causes of Difficult Behaviors
- Strategies for Working with Difficult Behaviors

Managing Workplace Conflict
- Causes of Conflict
- Conflict Management Styles
- Steps for Successful Conflict Management

Taking Disciplinary Action
- Focus on Behavior
- Disciplinary Options

Recap
Review Questions

6　Building a Team　　123

Why Teamwork?
- Organization Benefits
- Individual Benefits

What Is a Team?

Transforming a Group into a Team
- Share the Expectations
- Share the Responsibilities
- Share the Glory

Being a Valuable Team Member
- Use Active Listening
- Avoid Making Commitments You Can't Keep
- Deliver What You Promise
- Give Credit to Others
- Seek Contributions of Others
- Share Your Resources
- Work to Resolve Workplace Issues
- Keep Confidences
- Maintain a Sense of Humor
- Smile

Obstacles to Team Development
Recap
Review Questions

7 Getting the Work Done — 139

Performance Motivation
- Your Role in Motivation
- Different Folks, Different Strokes
- All Behavior Is Motivated

Obtaining Top Performance
- Establish and Communicate Expectations
- Provide Positive Feedback
- Focus on Teamwork
- Inspire, but Don't Control
- Lead by Example

Delegating to Get the Work Done
- Guidelines for Successful Delegation

Planning and Organizing for Success
- Imperatives of Planning
- Make Your Plan Specific, Achievable, and Measurable
- Plans Should Be in Writing
- Plans Must Have a Timetable
- Determine Priorities Beforehand
- Communicate What Is Going On
- Questions Your Plan Should Answer

Managing Your Time
- Use a Daily List of Things to Do
- Prioritize Your Daily List
- Determine the Best Use of Your Time Right Now
- Manage Your Time Like Money
- Strive for Life Balance with Your Time
- Effects of Stress on Productivity

Recap
Review Questions

8 Supervising in a Changing Environment — 161

Legal Issues for First-Line Supervisors
- Government Laws and Organization Policies
- Avoiding Legal Action

Supervising a Diverse Workforce
- Your Role in Supervising Diversity
- Developing Yourself for Diversity

The Distance Manager and Virtual Work
- What, Why, and When of Distance Management and Virtual Work
- Being a Successful Distance Manager
- Being a Successful Virtual Worker
- Organization Success Factors

Managing Change
    Stages of Change
    Managing Change as a First-Line Supervisor
Recap
Review Questions

9 Ensuring Your Success — 179
Reevaluate Your Confidence Level
Additional Skill Development
Ongoing Professional Development
Recap
Review Questions

Bibliography — 187
Post-Test — 193
Index — 199

FOR QUESTIONS AND COMMENTS:
Please contact Self Study at 1-800-225-3215 or email
AMASelfStudy@amanet.org for information about
Self Study courses. And visit our website at www.amaselfstudy.org

About This Course

Effective first-line supervision is critical to the success of nearly every organization. The ultimate execution of corporate plans and objectives rests at the supervisory level and depends on the supervisor's skills and abilities. This updated and revised fifth edition of *First-Line Supervision* prepares supervisors to develop the competencies required to translate the organization's goals at the front line.

As a first-time supervisor, your initial objective is to make the transition from staff member to supervisor, assuming the responsibilities of motivating, coaching, and leading your staff. This course will guide you in making the move to your new role, helping you identify your abilities and target skills to strengthen. Here you learn how to develop your own leadership style, understand the important personal qualities of an effective supervisor, build a strong team, and master techniques for getting the work done. The course focuses on developing the key competencies required for success in a changing business environment. It offers practical strategies for dealing with the daily realities of planning and conducting meetings, solving problems, crafting clear documents, training employees, and managing people, conflict, and change.

New to this edition is a chapter on supervising in a changing environment. The chapter features legal issues for supervisors, the challenges of supervising a diverse workforce, managing distant and virtual employees, and managing change. Added or expanded topics include developing a partnership with your boss, managing communication technology, providing performance feedback, working with difficult employees, and performance motivation.

First-Line Supervision, Fifth Edition, is designed to encourage you to apply these new skills to the job you are doing every day. You can use the exercises and assessments to work through your own supervisory challenges and hone the skills you need to be a dynamic and effective supervisor.

Charles M. Cadwell is the president of Training Systems +, based in Mulvane, Kansas, which specializes in training system design and development. He has more than twenty-five years of experience in the training field. Prior to starting Training Systems + in 1986, he held positions as Director of Field Training for Pizza Hut, Inc. and Director of Training for Popingo Video, Inc.

Cadwell's clients have included *Fortune* 500 companies as well as a number of small- and medium-size service, retail, and manufacturing businesses. In addition to developing training materials, he also frequently facilitates classroom training sessions.

His first book, *New Employee Orientation*, was published by Crisp Publications in 1988. Since then he has written three audiocassette programs for the American Management Association on the subjects of recruiting and selection, orientation and training, and leadership skills. He has also written four issues of the Trainer's Workshop for AMA. His most recent books are *How to Be an Effective Facilitator* (AMA, 1997), *Performance Management* (AMA, 2000), and *Leadership Skills for Managers*, Fourth Edition (AMA, 2004).

How to Take This Course

This course consists of text material for you to read and three types of activities (the Pre- and Post-Test, in-text exercises, and end-of-chapter Review Questions) for you to complete. These activities are designed to reinforce the concepts brought out in the text portion of the course and to enable you to evaluate your progress.

PRE- AND POST-TESTS

Both a pre-test and a post-test are included in this course. Take the pre-test before you study any of the course material to determine your existing knowledge of the subject matter. To get instructions on taking the test and having it graded, please email *AMASelfStudy@amanet.org*, and you will receive an email back with details on taking your test and getting your grade. This email will also include instructions on taking your post-test, which you should do upon completion of the course material.

CERTIFICATE

Once you have taken your post-test, you will receive an email with your grade and a certificate if you have passed the course successfully (70% or higher). All tests are reviewed thoroughly by our instructors, and your grade and a certificate will be returned to you promptly.

THE TEXT

The most important component of this course is the text, for it is here that the concepts and methods are first presented. Reading each chapter twice will increase the likelihood of your understanding the text fully.

We recommend that you work on this course in a systematic way. Only by reading the text and working through the exercises at a regular and steady pace will you get the most out of this course and retain what you have learned. In your first reading, concentrate on getting an overview of the chapter's contents. Read the learning objectives at the beginning of each chapter first. They serve as guidelines to the major topics of the chapter and enumerate the skills you should master as you study the text. As you read the chapter, pay attention to the headings and subheadings. Find the general theme of the section and see how that theme relates to others. Don't let yourself get bogged down with details during the first reading; simply concentrate on remembering and understanding the major themes.

In your second reading, look for the details that underlie the themes. Read the entire chapter carefully and methodically, underlining key points, working out the details of the examples, and making marginal notations as you go. Complete the exercises.

EXERCISES AND ACTIVITIES

Interspersed with the text in each chapter you will find exercises that take a variety of forms. In some cases, no specific or formal answers are provided. Where appropriate, suggested responses or commentary follow the chapters.

THE REVIEW QUESTIONS

After reading a chapter and before going on to the next, work through the review questions. By answering the questions and comparing your own answers to the answers provided, you will find it easier to grasp the major ideas of that chapter. If you perform these self-check exercises conscientiously, you will develop a framework in which to place material presented in later chapters.

QUESTIONS ABOUT GRADING/ RETAKING THE TEST

For those users who have purchased the online course, if you have questions regarding the tests, the grading, or the course itself, please email Self Study at *AMASelfStudy@amanet.org*.

If you fail the Post-Test, you have one year from the purchase date of your course to retake the test.

Pre-Test

First-Line Supervision
Fifth Edition

Course Code 90029

INSTRUCTIONS: *To take this test and have it graded, please email AMASelfStudy@amanet.org. You will receive an email back with details on taking your test and getting your grade.*

FOR QUESTIONS AND COMMENTS: *You can also contact Self Study at 1-800-225-3215 or visit the website at* www.amaselfstudy.org

1. When working with your boss it is best to:
   (a) tell your employees everything your boss tells you.
   (b) develop a partnership with clear expectations.
   (c) assume 50 percent of the responsibility for the relationship.
   (d) develop a relationship with your boss's boss.

2. When dealing with information, a first-line supervisor has to act as a(n) _____ between employees and upper management.
   (a) interpreter
   (b) insulation
   (c) gatekeeper
   (d) motivator

3. Part of the paradox of first-line supervision is explained by which of the following statements?
   (a) Supervisors are expected to get employees to work more hours.
   (b) Supervisors only have limited authority over employees.
   (c) Supervisors should not expect to make many decisions.
   (d) Supervisors need to be competent despite limited training.

4. Which factors do effective supervisors consider when choosing the most appropriate leadership style?
   (a) Availability, quality, experience
   (b) Availability, quality, time
   (c) Experience, time, information
   (d) Experience, information, quality

5. One of the primary reasons for companies to implement virtual work is to:
   (a) reduce overhead expenses.
   (b) reduce training costs.
   (c) outsource more work overseas.
   (d) reduce the need for supervision.

6. Because employees look to their supervisors for structure and direction, a first-line supervisor should:
   (a) handle problems and issues.
   (b) provide resources.
   (c) plan and organize work.
   (d) focus on administrative tasks.

7. The best way to develop your own listening habits is to:
   (a) stop the speaker as soon as something isn't clear.
   (b) hear the person out, and don't interrupt.
   (c) compare what is being said with what you already know.
   (d) be thinking of questions for the speaker.

8. The conflict management style that seeks the best for both parties is:
   (a) collaboration.
   (b) compromise.
   (c) avoidance.
   (d) accommodation.

9. The best orientation programs:
   (a) are completed the first day on the job.
   (b) involve the employee in planning the orientation.
   (c) ensure policy manuals are ready prior to beginning a task.
   (d) are developed and implemented by line management.

10. When coaching an employee whose performance has slipped, the first step is to:

(a) tell the person how to improve.
(b) get the person to tell you when improvement will be made.
(c) wait until the person comes to you and asks for help.
(d) get the employee to agree performance needs improvement.

11. Electronic messaging is best used for:
    (a) communicating confidential information.
    (b) normal day-to-day communication.
    (c) setting the stage for disciplinary action.
    (d) saying things you wouldn't say face-to-face.

12. When working with difficult employees it is best to focus on the employee's:
    (a) attitude.
    (b) attendance.
    (c) behavior.
    (d) home situation.

13. In order for employee feedback to be effective it should:
    (a) be specific and immediate.
    (b) focus on the negative first, the positive second.
    (c) be used sparingly so employees don't expect to get it.
    (d) be put in writing and a copy placed in the employee's file.

14. One thing you can do to make sure the training that your employees attend is effective is to:
    (a) have them pay for the training themselves.
    (b) send several people at one time.
    (c) have them attend on weekends or on days off.
    (d) recognize their improvement after the training.

15. The adjustment stage of the change process is frequently characterized by feelings of:
    (a) anger and numbness.
    (b) self-doubt and uncertainty.
    (c) contribution and commitment.
    (d) chaos and frustration.

16. Which of the following is characteristic of reverse delegation?
    (a) The supervisor reverses a bad decision when a problem occurs.
    (b) The supervisor winds up doing the work that was delegated.
    (c) The supervisor is able to identify resources that are needed.
    (d) The supervisor can select the best person to do a task.

17. Which of the following can be an obstacle to team development?
    (a) Being too busy with your own tasks

(b) Delegating too many tasks
(c) Asking employees for input too often
(d) Spending too much time coaching employees

18. Which of the following is the <u>best</u> thing you can do to help avoid legal action by employees?
    (a) Spend time learning the details of employment law.
    (b) Consult with legal counsel before taking disciplinary action.
    (c) Document your interactions with employees.
    (d) Reduce the amount of direct supervision of your employees.

19. Which of the following is true of the relationship between stress and productivity?
    (a) Stress lowers productivity.
    (b) Productivity lowers stress.
    (c) Some stress is necessary to be productive.
    (d) Most stress is harmful and causes work-related problems.

20. When supervising a diverse workforce it is important that you:
    (a) get direction from your boss on how to supervise.
    (b) ignore individual differences of opinion.
    (c) hire an equal number of males and females.
    (d) let people know where you stand on diversity.

21. The motivation factor that ranks highest for most employees is:
    (a) interesting work.
    (b) good pay.
    (c) recognition for a job well done.
    (d) tactful discipline.

22. The primary benefit of teamwork is that:
    (a) the manager does not have to work so hard.
    (b) people working together can accomplish more than individuals.
    (c) a team creates competition which increases productivity.
    (d) everyone enjoys being part of a team.

23. As a first-line supervisor, your time will be divided between working and supervising. Approximately how much of your time should you expect to spend supervising others?
    (a) 0–15 percent
    (b) 16–35 percent
    (c) 36–55 percent
    (d) 56–75 percent

24. Communication is most successful when:
    (a) the sender delivers a powerful message.
    (b) the receiver tries to listen effectively.

(c) the sender achieves specific results.
(d) the message is presented visually.

25. When taking disciplinary action you should:
    (a) always start by suspending the employee.
    (b) be glad that you have to take action.
    (c) involve as many employees as possible.
    (d) focus on the employee's behavior.

1

Becoming a Supervisor

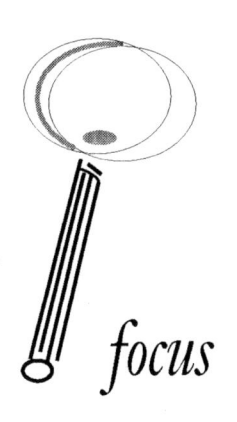

Learning Objectives

By the end of this chapter, you should be able to:

- Identify the requirements for making the transition from team member to first-line supervisor.
- List four reasons why first-line supervisors are important to an organization.
- Describe the paradoxes encountered by first-line supervisors.
- Explain what is meant by situational leadership.

When you are promoted to first-line supervisor, you become the boss. You may not be the "big boss" in charge of the whole organization, but you definitely have your own area of responsibility. Being the boss and being in charge brings with it many opportunities for success and failure. Now you're the one who has to worry about things that don't get done. Your responsibility goes beyond just putting in your time. You are responsible for results—your own results as well as those of your employees.

Dean Erskine looked around at his new workspace and began to think about what he was going to do now that he was in charge. He'd been waiting a long time for the opportunity. He felt he should have been promoted six months ago, when the boss picked LuAnne instead. He decided to give them another six months and, sure enough, just in the nick of time the company had finally seen the light or he would have been out the door. He would show them all now that they should have made the decision sooner. Today he would get his workspace organized, tomorrow he would begin changing the company.

MAKING THE TRANSITION TO FIRST-LINE SUPERVISOR

Dean seems confident that he is going to succeed as a supervisor. However, for many new supervisors this air of confidence is really used to mask genuine concern about themselves and their new responsibilities. First-line or first-time supervisors usually worry whether they have the qualities needed to be successful. For many, this is their first promotion, and they may have doubts about their ability to meet their new responsibilities and requirements. Take a few minutes to complete the following self-assessment to determine how prepared you are to make the transition to first-line supervisor.

✎ Exercise 1: Making the Transition: A Self-Assessment

INSTRUCTIONS: Read each of the statements below. On a scale of 1 to 10 (with 1 being "Not Confident" and 10 being "Very Confident"), circle the number that is nearest to your confidence level in making the transition from employee to first-line supervisor.

1. I can shift the focus from my area of technical or functional expertise to supervising other people.
    1   2   3   4   5   6   7   8   9   10

2. I can shift my focus from my job and my department to become aware of the entire organization and the role of individual departments and the relationships among departments.
    1   2   3   4   5   6   7   8   9   10

3. I can make the transition from being a doer to ensuring work gets done.
    1   2   3   4   5   6   7   8   9   10

4. I can handle multiple priorities at one time.
    1   2   3   4   5   6   7   8   9   10

5. I can shift my focus from the quality of my own performance to the quality and performance of the entire team.
    1   2   3   4   5   6   7   8   9   10

6. I can handle working the extra hours that may be required in my new role.
    1   2   3   4   5   6   7   8   9   10

7. I can make the transition from being an information receiver to being an information provider.
    1   2   3   4   5   6   7   8   9   10

8. I can make the transition from being concerned about my own personal satisfaction to a concern for motivating and developing my employees.
    1   2   3   4   5   6   7   8   9   10

9. I can make the transition from being a team member to being a team builder.

   1   2   3   4   5   6   7   8   9   10

10. I can maintain a positive attitude when more demands are placed on me.

    1   2   3   4   5   6   7   8   9   10

Add the numbers you circled for the ten statements.

Total Score: _____

Scoring

85-100: You are confident in your abilities and should be able to make a successful transition to first-line supervision.

70-85: You have some work to do as you make the transition.

Less than 70: Your score indicates that you are not sure about your ability to supervise others effectively. Use this course to provide yourself with the confidence to make a successful transition.

Exhibit 1-1 contrasts the issues listed in the self-assessment, showing what an employee does and what a supervisor does. Here's a brief summary of what those differences mean to a first-line supervisor.

Focus

Good employees have the skills required to do their jobs in an effective and productive manner. Their focus each day is on using their specific technical

Exhibit 1-1
Differences Between Employees and First-Line Supervisors

Employees Must:	First-Line Supervisors Must:
• Focus on their specific job skills	• Focus on supervising people
• Contribute to the department's success	• Contribute to the entire organization's success
• Do the work	• Ensure work gets done
• Work on specific priorities	• Be involved with multiple priorities
• Be most concerned about the quality of their own work	• Be concerned about the quality of the entire team's work
• Work a specified number of hours	• Be willing to work overtime and on a scheduled day off knowing there may not be any extra pay
• Receive information from others	• Share information with others
• Be personally motivated and satisfied	• Motivate and develop other employees
• Be an effective team member	• Be an effective team builder
• Have a good attitude, but can "get away" with having a bad attitude from time to time	• Maintain a positive attitude even when circumstances would make it easy to be negative

---

© American Management Association. All rights reserved.
http://www.amanet.org/

Exhibit 1-2

First-Line Supervision Time Allocation

	Executive	Supervisor	Employees
Supervising Others	80 to 95 percent	15 to 35 percent	0 to 5 percent
Using Technical Skills	5 to 20 percent	65 to 85 percent	95 to 100 percent

The higher one moves up the organization ladder, more time is spent supervising and less time using technical skills. At the executive level, managing and interacting with others may take as much as 80 to 95 percent of an executive's time and the direct use of technical skills may virtually be nonexistent. At the other end of the spectrum, employees will spend nearly 100 percent of their time using technical skills.

---

skills—such as engineering, accounting, or advertising. As a first-line supervisor, on the other hand, you will no longer spend all of your time using your technical skills, but instead you will be devoting a portion of your time to supervising your employees. Depending on the organization and the number of people in your work group, you may spend anywhere from 15 percent to 35 percent of your time supervising (see Exhibit 1–2).

Seeing the Big Picture

First-line supervisors have to move out from their little corner of the world and begin to see the big picture. You have to go beyond thinking about what's happening in your own department and begin to think about how your department's work contributes to the entire organization's success. In your new role, you will spend a considerable amount of time interacting with and learning to work with people from other parts of the organization.

The Work

Employees do the work and first-line supervisors ensure the work gets done. Although as a first-line supervisor you still have specific responsibilities of your own, you also assume responsibility for making sure your employees get their work done as well. To be effective you have to learn to split your time between doing your own specific tasks and following up on the work of your employees. Very often as a first-line supervisor you must function in both roles at the same time.

Number of Priorities

No matter how many priorities individual employees have, supervisors have responsibility for all the priorities of their employees. For example, say you have six people in your work group and each of them has four projects. You now have ultimate responsibility for twenty-four projects (6 times 4) plus any specific projects that you must complete by yourself. In other situations, all your employees may have the same ten major responsibilities and your job is to ensure that they all meet their responsibilities. These additional responsibilities and their associated time commitments can be a big challenge as you become a first-line supervisor.

Work Quality

Many new first-line supervisors are promoted because they are good at their specific employee job requirements. They are the best cook, best salesperson, best riveter, best electrical engineer, or the best accountant. You probably were good at your technical or functional responsibilities. In your new supervisory role you may have to work with people who are not as skilled as you are. As frustrating as this can be at first, you must resist the temptation to do the work for your employees. In the long run, you will be successful when you get your employees to produce work that meets your quality standards.

Time Commitment

Some employees may think that if they could just get promoted to first-line supervisor, their lives would be a whole lot easier. They would have more control over their work and time. In reality, the opposite is usually true. First-line supervisors normally have more demands placed on them and their time. A a result, they may spend most of their regular hours supervising and find that they have to stay late or come in early to get their own work done.

Dealing with Information

Employees typically are on the receiving end of information. They get the information that their supervisors share with them. In contrast, as a first-line supervisor you often become the "gatekeeper" of information because you are between your employees and upper management. You have to decide what information you receive from upper management that you communicate to your employees. Since complaints about communication (or lack of) dot the landscape of many organizations, to be effective you must learn how to deal with the information that comes your way.

Motivation

Chances are you were promoted to be a first-line supervisor because you were viewed as being self-motivated. The ability to keep yourself motivated is a positive attribute. Once promoted, it becomes your responsibility to motivate others as well as yourself. As a new supervisor, you must learn what motivates your employees and then provide them with the opportunity to motivate themselves and keep yourself motivated at the same time.

Role on the Team

Effective team members are important to every organization. Those who make the best individual contributions are often tapped to move up to first-line supervisor. In their new roles, they are expected to build teams with a variety of employees—not all of whom have the same degree of commitment that you have to do the best possible job. Transforming a group of individuals into a functional team presents its own set of challenges.

Attitude

Employees with positive attitudes are a plus in any organization. Those who can see the bright side of any situation can have a positive impact on those around them. New first-line supervisors normally assume their responsibilities with a positive attitude. As the realities of their new responsibilities become apparent, however, they become challenged to maintain the positive attitude they had when they were promoted. To be successful you have to learn to maintain a positive attitude—even during those times when you would rather vent your own frustrations—so your positive attitude rubs off on your employees.

✎ Exercise 2: Getting Ready to Make the Transition

INSTRUCTIONS: Now that you have read about the requirements for being a successful first-line supervisor, go back and review your score for each of the items on the self-assessment. Fill in your scores on the grid that follows. For each item where you had a score of seven or less, list what action you plan to take to improve your ability to make the transition to first-line supervisor. Sample responses are listed for each item.

Item	Score	Sample Action Required	Action Required
Focus		*Keep a time log for the first month to see how I'm spending my time.*	
Seeing the Big Picture		*Read the company's strategic plan and review department objectives.*	
The Work		*Avoid taking on responsibilities that employees should have.*	
Number of Priorities		*Make sure the department workload is balanced among all employees.*	
Work Quality		*Help people do quality work without expecting them to be perfect all the time.*	
Time Commitment		*Be flexible and open to working extra hours when necessary.*	
Dealing with Information		*Make a concerted effort to keep my employees informed without doing data dumps.*	
Motivation		*Use regular positive feedback to motivate my employees.*	

Item	Score	Sample Action Required	Action Required
Role on the Team		*Get employees working together so they feel part of a cohesive team.*	
Attitude		*Do my best not to bring home to work and vice versa.*	

IMPORTANCE OF FIRST-LINE SUPERVISION

As her department continued to grow, it became obvious to Denise that she needed to add a first-line supervisor in her records department. There were now fifteen clerks who needed more attention and assistance than she could provide. Plus, she was busy with the new projects that her boss, Kamel, had assigned her. She talked to him to get his perspective on the situation. After a couple of meetings he agreed with Denise and asked her to draw up a proposal for adding a first-line supervisor in the records department. Then they worked together to implement the change to make the whole department more productive.

Efficient and effective first-line supervision is one of the primary needs of practically every organization. In most cases, the ultimate execution of corporate plans and objectives comes down to the supervisory level and depends on the supervisor's skills and abilities. First-line supervisors are responsible for the results and performance that upper management needs for survival and growth. There are four reasons why first-line supervision is important:

1. Day-to-Day Operations
2. First Line of Contact for Employees
3. Span of Control
4. Development of Organization Talent

Day-to-Day Operations

Whether an organization's primary activity is wholesale, retail, hospitality, service, manufacturing, nonprofit, or some other type, the responsibility for day-to-day operations falls to first-line supervisors. If a customer or client has a problem, the first management person he or she comes in contact with is the first-line supervisor. The level of service and the quality of the work produced each day depends on the employees and the direction they receive from you—their first-line supervisor. This is where the "rubber meets the road" and where customers or clients develop their perceptions of an organization. You are the one who has to make it happen customer-by-customer and task-by-task if the organization is going to be successful.

First Line of Contact for Employees

If upper management wants to make a change in policy or procedure, first-line supervisors must introduce the change. If employees have questions about what the organization is doing, you need to know the answers or where to get them. The workforce's impression of the organization and of upper management is often a reflection of their impression of their first-line supervisor. Similarly, how employees treat customers or clients often reflects how the employees are treated by upper management. Thus, your actions as the first-line supervisor can have a significant impact on how customers and/or clients are treated and how they, in turn, perceive the organization.

Span of Control

First-line supervisors are needed to maintain an appropriate span of control. Although the span of control varies from organization to organization and from job to job, there is a point at which a person is needed to supervise either a certain number of employees or a certain number of tasks. When that point is reached, a first-line supervisor position is created. Even though there has been a trend in recent years to flatten organizations, most of the flattening has occurred at the middle management ranks. Effective first-line supervisors are always in demand in those organizations that want to maintain good customer and good employee relations.

Development of Organization Talent

First-line supervision is critical to the development of organization talent. In some cases, it is the first step up the management ladder. Success at the first level often leads to opportunities in middle management and perhaps ultimately to upper management. Organizations often use entry-level supervisory positions as "testing" grounds for those moving up in management. Though success at the first level may not necessarily translate into success higher up in the organization, failure at the first level is likely to mean failure at higher levels as well.

Even if you do not move up in the organization, the skills you develop as a first-line supervisor can help you maximize your own potential. Look at your new responsibilities as a development opportunity and take advantage of the situation to learn as much as you can about yourself and the organization. Demonstrate to those in upper management how you can have a positive impact when given even greater responsibilities. In the end, you will be a more valuable member of the organization regardless of your place in the hierarchy. This experience also gives you an advantage if you find yourself in a flatter organizational environment.

✎ Exercise 3: Having a Positive Impact as a First-Line Supervisor

INSTRUCTIONS: Think about each of the four reasons why first-line supervision is important. Write down some specific things that you can do to have a positive impact as a first-line supervisor. Sample responses are listed for each item.

1. Day-to-Day Operations
   Make sure my interactions with customers are handled in a professional manner that reflects positively on the company.

   _____

   _____

2. First Line of Contact
   Treat employees the way I want them to treat our customers.

3. Span of Control
   Be willing to handle a larger span of control if necessary.

4. Development of Organization Talent
   Read at least one supervisory management book each month to improve my knowledge and skills.

PARADOXES OF FIRST-LINE SUPERVISION

First-line supervisors face several paradoxes as they make the transition from being an employee to being in charge. Effective supervisors are aware of these paradoxes and are proactive in addressing them.

Being a Supervisor and a Technical Expert

The first paradox is that although you are now the supervisor of other people you are still expected to use your technical expertise. You have to find the right balance between supervising others and doing whatever technical work is still required of you. This can lead to frustration when you have trouble getting your own work done because of the supervisory issues that you have to address. It's not unusual for new supervisors to feel more at home doing the technical work than in performing their new supervisory tasks. So when push comes to shove, they elect to focus on the technical tasks that are more familiar. For people like Pat, this only further complicates the problem.

   Pat had waited for a long time for a promotion to a supervisory position in her department. She was good with people and good with the technical things that needed to be done. She knew she could manage the projects she had now as well as oversee other people's projects. That would have been fine if there had been no new projects. However, her boss continued to bring her new projects. Pat looked around at her team and decided they were too busy to take on something new. She also knew the expectations of her boss so she decided to tackle the new projects herself. In less than a month she was overwhelmed and wound up working overtime every week. Meanwhile her people were waiting for her to assist them on their own projects—but she didn't have time to help them.

Unfortunately there are no hard and fast rules you can follow as a supervisor. However, you can do some things to help you sort through this paradox. First, don't take on responsibility for doing everything yourself. When a new project comes your way, assign it to one of your staff and put him or her in charge. Second, recognize that you can use your expertise to help others. Instead of doing so many things yourself, help others develop their own skills by sharing your expertise with them. Third, develop your time management skills. Determine what you can and should be doing to be most effective. Don't schedule your time so tight that you fail to allow time for handling supervisory issues.

Little Effort Is Devoted to Training

The second paradox is that although competent management is needed, often not enough effort is devoted to training supervisors and improving their management and leadership skills. Since supervisors are expected to be primarily task oriented, the emphasis frequently is on getting the job done and not on learning better management and leadership skills.

Rather than waiting for someone to provide training, be proactive and make it your own responsibility to learn all you can about your new role. Several books are listed in the Bibliography of this course that you may find helpful. Be on the lookout for books that focus on some of the specific skills for improving the effectiveness of first-line supervisors.

Getting the most out of people is not easy, nor is it done by merely giving orders. Regardless of your present level of experience, there is always room to improve your supervisory skills. Seminars and training courses can also assist you. You can overcome this paradox by taking the initiative to develop your supervisory skills.

The Way Work Is Organized

A third paradox is evident in the way a first-line supervisor's work is organized. The emphasis is frequently on "getting the work out," and the goals are expressed in terms of quotas, standards, units, or some measure of productivity or performance. Some businesses place the emphasis on getting out new products, bringing in new customers, or providing quality customer service. The fact is that things get done through the efforts of people. As a result, the development of people skills may not be given enough emphasis when preparing first-line supervisors to assume their new responsibilities.

As with the training paradox, the key is to be proactive. Though you may not be involved in setting organizational goals, budgeting, or making many other managerial decisions, as a first-line supervisor you are always involved with the day-to-day operations that directly affect an organization's product or service. Do what you can to ensure the work is organized in a manner than enables you and your team to be most efficient and effective.

Supervising Tasks and Learning Skills

A fourth paradox is that you must constantly choose between supervising specific job tasks and learning new skills. You also have to decide how much time to spend on each area. There are literally hundreds of questions and only a limited number of resources you can turn to. In the end, a great deal of your success depends on your own efforts at self-development.

Use the results of the self-assessment you completed earlier (Exercise 1–1) to identify the skills you need to develop. Determine where you can put your efforts to get the most return on the time and energy you invest. Look at self-development as just that—an investment. What you learn and the skills you develop now will pay future dividends. Don't wait. The sooner you invest in your own self-development, the sooner you'll reap the rewards.

Exercise 4: Addressing the Paradoxes of First-line Supervision

INSTRUCTIONS: What can you do to proactively address the paradoxes just described? Take a few minutes to write down some specific actions you can take. Sample responses are listed for each item.

1. Being a Supervisor and a Technical Expert
   Remember to allow time in my schedule for supervisory tasks as well as technical tasks.

   _____

   _____

   _____

2. Little Effort Devoted to Training
   Be aware of supervisory training classes that are offered and ask to attend those that would be beneficial.

   _____

   _____

   _____

3. The Way Work Is Organized
   Keep focused on my relationship with my employees as well as how much work they get done.

   _____

   _____

   _____

4. Supervising Tasks and Learning Skills
   Take the initiative to develop myself by asking questions of other experienced, successful supervisors.

   _____

   _____

   _____

LEADERSHIP STYLE AND BEHAVIOR

You have just learned what it takes to be an effective first-line supervisor and the importance of the first-line supervisor's role. Also, you are now aware of the paradoxes, or challenges, associated with being a first-line supervisor. The next thing you need to consider is, "How do I want to supervise others?" In other words, what leadership style do you want to adopt? Leadership *style* refers to the general way you deal with your work group. Some supervisor-leaders are authoritarian and domineering, others are supportive and participative. There is no absolutely correct style. Your style is determined partly by your personality and partly by how effectively you can adapt to various situations.

Your first inclination may be to adopt the style of a previous boss whom you respected or admired. If that person's style seemed to get results, that style may be the logical way to supervise. If you consider your previous boss to be a bad example, you may have learned only what not to do, rather than what to do. Either way, if your style is rigidly based on what you have observed in others, problems may arise if the situation changes. A style that works in one situation may not get the job done in another.

Task vs. People

As a first-line supervisor you are responsible for getting the work done through your people. How you approach that responsibility is a reflection of your leadership style. Some supervisors put more emphasis on getting the work done and less emphasis on their relationships with people. These supervisors are said to have a *task-oriented* leadership style. A lot of work gets done, but sometimes with a negative impact on morale and interpersonal relationships.

Other supervisors put more emphasis on their relationships with their people and less emphasis on getting the job done. These supervisors have a *people-oriented* leadership style. They have a lot of happy people working for them, but not much work gets accomplished; what does get accomplished may not always be of the best quality.

Whether you tend to be more task-oriented or more people-oriented affects the way you supervise others. How you supervise others also has an impact on your employees and the quality and quantity of work that is getting done.

Exercise 5: What's Your Leadership Style?

INSTRUCTIONS: Read each of the statements below. Circle the number on the scale from 1 to 10 that best reflects how you would behave in the situation described.

I explain exactly how I want the work to be done.		I let people make suggestions on how to do the job.
	1 2 3 4 5 6 7 8 9 10	
My primary concern is getting the job done.		My primary concern is how people feel about their work.
	1 2 3 4 5 6 7 8 9 10	
I establish the standards for people.		I let the people set their own standards.
	1 2 3 4 5 6 7 8 9 10	
I make the decisions for my work group.		I let people make their own decisions.
	1 2 3 4 5 6 7 8 9 10	
I tell people how much time they have to complete a task.		I ask people to tell me how long a task will take.
	1 2 3 4 5 6 7 8 9 10	
I expect people to ask me questions before they act.		I expect people to answer their own questions.
	1 2 3 4 5 6 7 8 9 10	
I expect people to make work their first priority.		I understand people have things to do that are more important than work.
	1 2 3 4 5 6 7 8 9 10	
I want frequent progress reports about work status.		I only want to know when a job is completed.
	1 2 3 4 5 6 7 8 9 10	
The less discussion about a job the better.		I like thorough discussions before work starts.
	1 2 3 4 5 6 7 8 9 10	
I expect people to be working with minimal socializing.		It's okay for people to socialize while they are working.
	1 2 3 4 5 6 7 8 9 10	

Add the numbers you have circled for the ten statements.

    Total Score: _____

© American Management Association. All rights reserved.
http://www.amanet.org/

Scoring

0-35: You tend to be more task-oriented and want to make sure the job is done they way you want it done.

36-69: You tend to have a balanced leadership style. You want to get the job done, but you are also concerned about people.

70-100: You tend to be more people-oriented. You give people more freedom in deciding what to do and how to do it.

Are you more task-oriented or more people-oriented? People who are extremely task-oriented are likely to be those who provide a lot of direction, make most of the decisions, and keep things under tight control. Their unspoken phrase is "my way or the highway." People who are extremely people-oriented, on the other hand, may appear to be wishy-washy. They may avoid making decisions for fear of making someone unhappy. They want the group to make the decisions. Their unspoken phrase is "do whatever you think is best." Supervisors who rely on either of these extremes will likely experience problems because using the same style all the time and with all people is not effective.

Generally, the best leadership style is one that is balanced—where there is a concern for both getting the job done and taking care of the people. A balanced approach requires choosing a leadership style that takes into account the needs of the employee and the circumstances at any given time. The effective supervisor recognizes that there are times when a task-oriented approach is best and there are other times when a people-oriented approach is best. Their choice of a leadership style depends on three primary factors: experience level, information available, and time available.

Experience Level

How much experience your employees have should influence your choice of a leadership style. For example, a new employee who has little or no experience about a job needs more direction and guidance than an experienced employee. With new employees, you normally need to be more task-oriented. They want and need to be provided with lots of direction. On the other hand, experienced employees can resent being told exactly how to do a job, especially if they have developed their own methods based on their experience. A more people-oriented leadership style would probably be more appropriate with experienced employees.

Information Available

You also should consider how much information is available regarding the job. Are all the facts, figures, and expectations well known or are there lots of unanswered questions? Is the job similar to one that has been done before? Are the standards clear? Is there a definite time when it has to be done? If the employee is unable to answer these questions, a more task-oriented approach would be best because more direction will be required to get the job done correctly. However, if there are few questions and the standards are clear, you can allow the employee more latitude in deciding how to get the job done.

Time Available

The third consideration is how much time is available to get the job done. If there is a short turnaround time you may need to take a more task-oriented approach and make most of the decisions yourself. There may not be enough time to discuss alternatives or involve other people in making decisions. You will have to decide what to do and how to do it. If you are not under pressure to get the job done immediately, you can take time to get input from your people. They may be able to provide suggestions on how best to get the job done. As you consider the time factor, keep in mind the old saying, "Haste makes waste." In some cases, even when you have a short time frame to get a job done, you may want to invest part of that time getting input from your people. If they have some say in what is to be done, they are likely to be more committed to helping you get it done in the time available.

In the end, your leadership style depends on how you view your people and the task to be done. When possible, take a balanced approach that matches the needs and skills of the employees with your preferred leadership style. Exhibit 1–3 shows the relationship among the factors to consider when selecting a leadership style.

Other Considerations Affecting Leadership Style

First-line supervisors usually have questions about how hard or easy they should be in dealing with their employees. In addition, there is usually considerable pressure from superiors to "Get the job done and don't worry about offending someone." You will see rude, rough people succeeding and sin-

Exhibit 1–3
Selecting a Leadership Style

The extremes of the task-oriented and people-oriented styles are described below. Effective supervisors don't choose their style based on their own personal whims. Instead, they consider the experience, information, and time available before they decide which leadership style will be most successful.

Task-Oriented	*Balanced*	*People-Oriented*
• The task is most important • Do it my way • I'll show and tell you what I want • I know what's best • My way or the highway	Make a decision after considering the effect of: • Experience • Information • Time	• People should be happy at work • What do you want to do? • Do what you think will work best • Anything is okay with me
Goal: To get the job done the way the leader wants it done.	Goal: To get the job done and take care of people at the same time.	Goal: To keep the people happy and hope that the job gets done.

cere, nice people failing. You will likely hear comments such as "Nice guys finish last" and " Winning is the only thing."

Keep in mind that there is a middle ground in most situations. The best advice is to be yourself and don't forget that you need your employees to get the job done. Your people want and need you to be an effective leader. In the long run, learning to adapt your style to different employees and different situations will help you achieve the results you want.

Here are three things you should consider when selecting your leadership style:

1. Delegation Skill
2. Organizational Constraints
3. Power Centers and Formal Structure

Delegation Skill
Few things are more important than developing the ability to delegate effectively. Like most new supervisors you may have difficulty deciding exactly what should and should not be delegated. When under pressure to complete a job, you may decide that it would be quicker to do it yourself. If this happens, a delegation opportunity is lost, and the chance to develop your leadership skills is forfeited. A lost delegation opportunity is also a missed opportunity to build employee competence and skills.

Organizational Constraints
You have to be aware of the predominant leadership style in your work environment. The nature of the organization also influences how you are expected to supervise. Learn to work within those organizational constraints and develop a leadership style that enables you to bring out the best in others and to deliver quality work.

For example, if the organization is critical of mistakes and failures, people will avoid risks. In this situation, focus on learning and continuous improvement. This enables you to help others see mistakes as learning opportunities and encourage them to try new things without fear. If your organization wants to maintain the status quo, focus on helping people master their current job and use crosstraining to build greater skill breadth. This provides an opportunity for you to use your coaching and delegation skills for personal growth and to build organizational capability.

If the organization is highly "change" oriented, there may not always be procedures to follow; innovative leadership may be a prized commodity. Organizations that encourage internal competition need first-line supervisors who provide coaching and supportive leadership. As a coach, you help employees focus on doing high quality work and support their progress. As a supporter, you help your team make good decisions that are in the best interest of the organization, the customers, and the team.

Power Centers and Formal Structure
Power centers are the people within the organization who shape its informal attitudes. In different organizations, certain departments have varying

degrees of power. Depending on what drives the organization-sales, marketing, accounting, or production—that group may predominate.

Your influence may be affected by what the power centers within the organization normally allow to happen. You have to be very clear about the effect of your group on other areas. Where there is a lot of internal conflict, the supervisor often gets caught up in other people's warfare. Be extra careful in these situations; you may win a battle and lose a war.

Be very sure that your personal and group goals are aligned with those of your boss. Don't get involved in high-level warfare. Identify what is most important and concentrate your efforts in that direction. In hostile organization environments, there may be only limited opportunities for leadership. Under these circumstances, performance and productivity mainly depend on the amount of interdepartmental cooperation necessary to get the work done.

✎ Exercise 6: Leadership Style Considerations

INSTRUCTIONS: Based on your knowledge of your organization and your own leadership preferences, what will you consider when choosing your leadership style? What action can you take to minimize any negative impact these considerations might have on your style? One example is given to get you started.

Factors Affecting Your Style	Action You Plan to Take
Wanting to do it myself	*Take time necessary to train employees so I can delegate work to them rather than doing it all myself.*
_____	_____
_____	_____
_____	_____

recap

This chapter lays the foundation for making the transition from employee to first-line supervisor. Several important issues were discussed. First, you must be prepared to make the transition to first-line supervisor. Your confidence in being able to make the transition can affect your potential for success as a first-line supervisor.

Second, you need to be aware of the importance of first-line supervisors to an organization. They perform several valuable functions such as supervising the day-to-day operations, being the first line of contact for employees, impacting the span of control, and developing themselves for middle and upper management positions.

Third, first-line supervisors must deal with the paradoxes that go along with the job. For example, you are expected to be a supervisor and use your technical expertise at the same time. Second, although management and supervisory skills are required, often very little formal training is provided. Also, the way the work is organized often puts a premium on getting the work out rather than preparing first-line supervisors for their new responsibilities. In the end supervisors often have to choose between supervising specific tasks and learning new skills.

And fourth, we discussed the issue of leadership style. Successful supervisors select a leadership style that takes into account both the task to be done and the people involved. They try to take a balanced approach whenever possible that considers the experience of their employees, the amount of information available, and the time available. The most successful supervisors try to match their preferred leadership style with the needs and skills of their employees.

Exercise 7: Taking It Back to the Workplace

INSTRUCTIONS: Now that you have completed the reading and the activities in this chapter, it's time to think specifically about how to apply what you have learned. The following questions are designed to help you consider what you need to do to succeed back in the workplace.

- ❑ Have you developed an action plan for making the transition to first-line supervision?
- ❑ Have you identified what you need to do to have a positive impact in your new role?
- ❑ Are you ready to deal with the paradoxes of being a first-line supervisor? What will you do?
- ❑ What adjustments do you need to make to your leadership style?

Review Questions

INSTRUCTIONS: *Here is the first set of review questions in this course. Answering the questions following each chapter gives you a chance to check your comprehension of the concepts as they are presented and reinforces your understanding of them.*

As you can see below, the answer to each numbered question is printed to the side of the question. Before beginning, you should conceal the answers in some way, either by folding the page vertically or by placing a sheet of paper over the answers. Then read and answer each question. Compare your answers with those given. For any questions you answer incorrectly, make an effort to understand why the answer given is the correct one. You may find it helpful to turn back to the appropriate section of the chapter and review the material of which you are unsure. At any rate, be sure you understand all the review questions before going on to the next chapter.

1. How much time do new first-line supervisors typically spend supervising their employees?
   (a) 5 to 25 percent
   (b) 15 to 35 percent
   (c) 25 to 45 percent
   (d) 35 to 55 percent

   1. (b)

2. The phrase "where the rubber meets the road" refers to:
   (a) the supervisor's responsibility for day-to-day operations.
   (b) the supervisor being the first line of contact for employees.
   (c) having the right span of control to ensure happy customers.
   (d) the supervisor moving up the organization ladder.

   2. (a)

3. Which of the following is a paradox of first-line supervision?
   (a) Training your employees to do their jobs
   (b) Developing your people skills necessary to be successful
   (c) Having goals and objectives expressed in quotas, standards, and units
   (d) Deciding between helping an employee develop skills and working on a project

   3. (d)

4. Which leadership style would be most appropriate to use when making a job assignment to a new employee?
   (a) Task-oriented
   (b) People-oriented
   (c) Balanced
   (d) Any leadership style can be used with new employees

4. (a)

5. Which of the following is an example of an organizational constraint that can affect your ability to lead?
   (a) Upper management's approach to the business
   (b) Your own attitude toward the job
   (c) The length of time it takes to be promoted
   (d) Your experience in supervising others

5. (a)

2

Role of the Supervisor

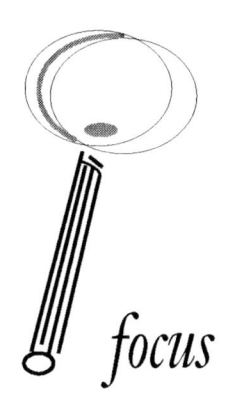

Learning Objectives

By the end of this chapter, you should be able to:

- Identify and describe the roles of a first-line supervisor.
- List the personal qualities of an effective first-line supervisor.
- Explain how best to work with your boss.
- Describe the six key competencies for effective first-line supervision.

Stephen was ready for his first meeting with his team as their new supervisor. He waited until five minutes past the planned starting time to enter the conference room. He wanted to make a grand entrance and let everyone know he was in charge. He was surprised when the room didn't become quiet immediately after he walked in. He was also surprised that not everyone was there—where was Eileen? Not to be deterred, he took a seat at the front of the room and said, "Let's get down to business. As you know, I'm Stephen and I'm your new supervisor. I plan to make this group more productive than you have ever been before. Today I will outline my plan and what I expect from you. First, don't call me Steve or something stupid like Stevie—my name is Stephen. You can either address me as Stephen or as Mr. Warren. No exceptions. Does everyone understand?" As he looked around the room, he could see some surprised and even concerned looks on the faces of some of his employees. Apparently they were getting the message that things were going to change. There was a new boss and he was the one.

Some first-line supervisors, when they get promoted, suddenly think they know everything there is to know. These supervisors also think that their employees will automatically do everything asked of them. They make themselves the center of attention and seem to quickly lose sight of their people. Stephen was taking that approach and even though he could see some signs of concern, he had his mind made up and was ready to move full steam ahead on his planned path—because he was the boss.

Successful first-line supervisors know that they have to earn the respect of their people before they will be fully accepted as the boss. In order to be successful, you have to do more than just hold the title of supervisor if you want the respect of your people. You must understand the need for knowledge, for setting a good example, and for gaining experience.

Nothing builds respect better than demonstrating your *knowledge* to your employees. They want to know that you know what you are doing. Chances are, one of the reasons you were promoted was because of your job knowledge. As a first-line supervisor you will often work side by side with your employees. Being knowledgeable gives you power. In describing their best supervisors, employees often say, "They really know their stuff."

Knowledge alone, however, is not enough. You also have to set a *positive example* for your employees. You have to "walk the walk" as well as "talk the talk." In other words, just knowing what to do isn't enough. You have to be able to perform as well. Your employees will watch what you do. If they see you taking shortcuts to get the job done, they assume it's okay for them to take shortcuts as well. Effective first-line supervisors know that telling their people, "Do as I say, not as I do," won't work for long, if at all.

The added ingredient of *experience*, along with knowledge and setting a good example, will help make you an effective first-line supervisor. Experience comes from doing the job consistently and learning from what you do right as well as from what you do wrong. Effective supervisors are usually quick learners. They don't make the same mistake twice. They learn from their mistakes, but don't dwell on them. They move forward and make sure that next time things are done correctly.

Day-to-Day Supervisory Roles

Once you have the knowledge, set a positive example, and gain experience, it's your day-to-day actions that define you as a good boss or a bad one. There are five actions that effective first-line supervisors consistently take:

1. Plan and Organize Work
2. Provide Resources
3. Manage and Develop People
4. Administer and Control
5. Handle Problems and Issues

Plan and Organize Work

People need to know what you expect them to do. It's your responsibility to plan and organize their work. Employees look to you for structure and direction; you have to be ready to provide both. Effective supervisors have a clear picture of what needs to be done and why, and they are able to communicate it clearly to their employees.

Provide Resources

It's your job to make sure your employees have the tools and supplies they need to get their jobs done. If you're on top of your job, in most cases you should know when your people need something; even better, you should know ahead of time. Don't wait for your employees to come to you. By then it may be too late, and you'll have to delay a project until you get the necessary supplies.

Manage and Develop People

Each day you are expected to manage and develop people. Effective supervisors know how to get the most out of their people. They view their employees as their most important asset. They understand that an important part of managing people means helping them do their jobs. They also know that developing their people to their fullest potential makes their employees more productive and enables the whole team to achieve more. Remember, if your employees are successful, you are successful.

Administer and Control

Numerous administrative tasks will take up your time each day. Although they vary from organization to organization, some of the most common are scheduling, keeping track of absences or tardiness, responding to requests, and completing required reports. The records you maintain help you keep track of what is happening today and provide control over the longer term. The regular completion of these tasks also communicates to your employees that you are aware of and monitoring their day-to-day activities.

Handle Problems and Issues

Nearly every day a supervisor has to handle some problem or issue. It may be an employee who doesn't show up for work or an employee who isn't doing the job properly. Conflicts between employees can also hamper the effectiveness of the team. First-line supervisors are expected to be proactive and handle problems and issues before they get out of control. Good supervisors generally deal with fewer performance problems and issues because they are aware of what's on the minds of their employees. They also handle the situation at the first level, so it doesn't have to go on up the management ladder.

✎ Exercise 1: Day-to-Day Supervisory Roles

INSTRUCTIONS: Think about each of the five roles described in this section. Take a moment to identify some specific actions you can take to be an effective first-line supervisor.

1. Plan and Organize Work
   (a) What can you do to ensure that all employees know what they need to accomplish?

   _____
   _____
   _____

   (b) What can you do to help employees organize their work so they can be productive?

   _____
   _____
   _____

2. Provide Resources
   (a) What resources do your employees need to get the job done?

   _____
   _____
   _____

   (b) What are the benefits of providing these resources?

   _____
   _____
   _____

   (c) What are the negative consequences of not providing these resources?

   _____
   _____
   _____

3. Manage and Develop People
   (a) What can you do to effectively manage your people each day?

   _____
   _____
   _____

   (b) What steps are you taking to help your people develop their potential?

   _____
   _____
   _____

(c) How do you communicate to your employees that they are important?

___

___

___

4. Administer and Control
   (a) What administrative tasks are you required to do each day? Each month?

   ___

   ___

   ___

   (b) How much control do you have over what is happening?

   ___

   ___

   ___

   (c) What are you doing so that you are viewed as in control, but not over controlling?

   ___

   ___

   ___

5. Handle Problems and Issues
   (a) What seems to be the primary source of supervisor problems and issues?

   ___

   ___

   ___

   (b) How can you be proactive in handling problems and issues?

   ___

   ___

   ___

   (c) What can you do to decrease the amount of time you spend handling problems and issues?

   ___

   ___

   ___

Personal Qualities of an Effective First-Line Supervisor

Stephen Warren, whom you met earlier in this chapter, created a somewhat negative first impression with his team by the way he approached his first meeting as a supervisor. He seemed to expect his employees to look up to him and respect him merely because of his new position. His self-centered attitude was probably obvious to all those in the room—except himself. Had he taken another approach, the tone would have been quite different. He could have started by asking his employees to tell him a little bit about themselves and what they expected. He could have engaged in some "small talk" to break the ice instead of just wanting to immediately get down to business. These may seem like small things, but they can make a difference in the success of a new supervisor.

Effective first-line supervisors must possess certain personal qualities that enable them to gain and maintain both the trust and respect of their employees. These personal qualities provide a foundation on which supervisors can build a mutually beneficial relationship with their employees. These qualities should be evident to your employees as you perform the day-to-day supervisory roles discussed earlier. In addition, these qualities must be consistently and continually obvious to those around you. As you read this section, think about how you measure up to these personal qualities and what changes, if any, you need to make.

Set High Personal Standards

People want to follow someone they can believe in. You must set an example for others to follow, and display a sincere, honest concern for quality and high performance. Invariably the group's activities reflect your standards and example. What people see in your conduct is what you receive in return. If you want respect, you have to respect the people who work for you. Emotional outbursts, unbecoming behavior, poor manners, or unethical conduct on your part detract from your ability to supervise. Instead, be certain that you practice ethical conduct, maintain an even temper, and use respectful language regardless of the situation. In short, role model the kind of behavior you want from your employees.

Be Accessible

Keep an open door policy. Let employees know that you welcome their suggestions and even their complaints. Be available whenever they want to talk to you. Listen to what they say. Often some of the best ideas come from the people doing the job, not the person supervising the job. Put into practice the communication techniques you learn in this course to ensure you don't have communication breakdowns.

Don't sit in your office and look at reports all day. Go wherever your employees are and talk to them. Find out what they are doing and help them if they are having problems. When you find good work, compliment your employees on their efforts. People like to be recognized for what they do—especially by the boss.

Inspire Success

Inspire people with the believability of success. All too few people believe they can be winners. Help your people believe in their own ability. Effective supervisors constantly emphasize that success is expected and de-emphasize the difficulty in reaching goals.

Deal with performance by displaying a constant commitment to quality and responsibility. Develop the belief that things will get better for everyone if they work together. Initially you may have to set up easy-win situations to develop self-confidence. Then you can progress to worthwhile challenges. Recognize satisfactory performance, not just the exceptional.

Constantly re-emphasize the value of the work. Involve people in mutual goals of self-respect, personal responsibility, and pride in their work. Show them that what they do relates to their own personal goals. Develop the idea of value in doing a job well. Encourage people to think of the product they are developing or the service they are providing as being done for themselves.

Accept Responsibility for Your Actions

No matter how hard you try, you will make mistakes. Something will go wrong. You will be asked to explain your actions. How you respond when things don't go as planned is a reflection of your maturity. Your response may also provide others with one way of assessing your ability to move up in the organization.

When things go wrong, you have to be willing to accept responsibility for your decisions and actions. Don't be afraid to admit you made a mistake. Most people understand that mistakes do happen. Instead of finding someone to blame, your boss most likely will want to know, "What did you learn from your mistake?" and "What can you do so it doesn't happen again?" The worst approach you can take is to deny that you made a mistake or to try and make someone else the scapegoat.

Sometimes a mistake made by one of your employees will reflect on you and your supervision. Even if you weren't directly responsible for the mistake, you have to be willing to accept your share of the responsibility. Somewhere along the line your action or inaction contributed to the mistake. Perhaps your communication wasn't clear or maybe you forgot to follow up on the employee's work. Accepting responsibility in these situations can help your relationship with all those you work with—your boss, your peers, and your employees.

Emphasize Quality and Service

Effective supervisors place great emphasis on quality and service. They focus on the things that give meaning to work and display empathy toward what has to be done. Define what your product or service does for others.

Identify for team members how others need and depend on the work the team does. Just as quality and service are two of the most important things that people look for in the marketplace, quality and service within an organization are critical to long-term success. Developing a quality and service emphasis among your work team is a priority for those who want to be effective first-line supervisors.

Believe in Employees

Make sure your entire work group knows that you believe that strong employees are a benefit and not a threat. If you encourage participation by delegating and training, your employees will be more willing to accept you as their supervisor.

Indicate that you want people to be self-reliant and self-disciplined. Encourage your staff to accept personal responsibility. Effective supervisors constantly challenge their people to reach high, achievable goals. You do this by letting your employees know that you believe in them and their capabilities.

The best supervisors communicate and reflect their individual concerns and values and the purpose of their organization to the group. They willingly accept feedback and provide feedback to ensure that people are listening and that they understand what is being communicated. Effective supervisors reflect the common concerns of their group, as well as the goals of the organization.

The fact that you are interested in and concerned for your people's development can do wonders to strengthen your supervisory role. You may have employees who do not want to grow beyond a certain level or leave their comfort zone. In most cases, however, your employees will strive for improvement if they know you believe in them. Your job as a supervisor is to provide every opportunity possible to train, teach, or encourage those individuals who are interested in personal development.

Set Priorities and Stick to Them

People want and expect a manager to be decisive about important things. By keeping the focus on the major concerns and not on minor issues, you demonstrate your personal involvement and commitment.

Supervisors often impair their ability to be successful by focusing first-rate energy on second-rate concerns. By implying that all issues are equally important, and attempting to control and direct everything, they abdicate responsibility. When many things are started and only a few are completed, supervisors confuse their people.

At times you will receive contradictory or unreasonable demands from upper management. If you can tactfully and unemotionally define the limits of the possible and impossible, you will have the chance to develop yourself as an effective supervisor in the eyes of your people. Never forget, however, to acknowledge as cheerfully as possible the ultimate authority of upper management. Your job is not to lead a revolt, but to ensure that upper management and your people understand one another and work toward the same goal.

Strive for Continuous Improvement

Effective first-line supervisors recognize that there is always room for improvement. They look for ways to make things better or to make improvements, even when everyone else is satisfied with their efforts and results. They are rarely satisfied with the status quo.

Your willingness to be your own worst critic is an important quality. If you are "tough" on yourself, most of the negative comments you hear from others will pale in comparison. In fact, if you develop a reputation for closely scrutinizing your own work, there will be less reason for others to do so. When people realize that you want to do what's best, they will get behind you and support your efforts.

✎ Exercise 2: Using Your Personal Qualities

INSTRUCTIONS: Take a moment to consider each of the personal qualities described in this section. In the middle column, write a brief description of how you measure up to each quality. In the right column, describe what changes, if any, you need to make when you are working with others so the quality is evident in your actions.

Personal Quality	How Do You Measure Up?	Changes Required
Set High Personal Standards		
Be Accessible		
Inspire Success		
Accept Responsibility for Your Actions		
Emphasize Quality and Service		
Believe in Employees		
Set Priorities and Stick to Them		
Strive for Continuous Improvement		

WORKING WITH YOUR BOSS

For Michelle Vaughn getting promoted was, in her view, a double victory. First, she would now be able to call some of the shots. Second, she would no longer have to put up with Dean Canton as her boss. She hadn't met her new boss yet, but he couldn't be any worse than what she had been dealing with for the past year. Michelle had already decided that the best course of action would be to take the initiative and do things her way. That would show her new boss that she was capable and would not be a bother. If he wanted to talk to her, she would always be willing to listen. Right now, however, she wanted to focus on her priorities and get things moving in the right direction.

When you are promoted to first-line supervision, your initial thoughts are likely to be focused on yourself and what *you* will be doing. You may not give too much thought to your boss—other than thinking about his or her excellent decision-making for recognizing your ability and selecting you for your new supervisory assignment. This is a mistake. The truth is your boss is a very important person to you—just as you are to your boss. Developing and maintaining a positive working relationship with your boss will pay many dividends as you deal with the day-to-day challenges of your supervisory responsibilities. Even if you have the same boss you had before getting promoted, there is likely to be some change in the relationship because of the different situation.

Keep in mind that your boss has a boss too. Just as you may sometimes feel pressure from your boss, you can be sure your boss is also feeling pressure from above. Since your boss is one step higher up the ladder, the pressure is likely a little heavier than what you are feeling. Recognizing this can help you have empathy for your boss. Just as you have to spend a lot of time helping the people who report to you, your boss has to do the same thing for the people who report to him or her—and you're just one of those people. There may be times when you feel like your boss isn't giving you the support you need. Before you become critical of your boss, ask yourself, "Am I giving all the people who report to me the support they need?" Likewise, ask yourself, "Am I giving my boss all the support he or she needs from me?"

The more attuned you are to your boss's situation, the easier it is for you to do your part to develop a mutually beneficial relationship. Exhibit 2–1 shows the four things you can proactively do:

- Develop a Partnership
- Focus on Common Priorities
- Communicate Upward
- Maximize the Relationship Potential

Exhibit 2–1
Working with Your Boss

Developing a positive working relationship with your boss should start as soon as you get promoted and continue as long as you work together. The key elements of developing a mutually beneficial relationship are shown here. It is not necessary to work on these in any specific order, in fact, you may work on them all simultaneously.

Develop a Partnership	Focus on Common Priorities
Communicate Upward	Maximize the Relationship Potential

Develop a Partnership

People enter into partnerships because they believe they can benefit from the strengths of others. In a good partnership, all parties recognize what contributions they can make to others and in turn, they recognize what they can gain from others. In a legal partnership arrangement, formal written documents spell out the roles and responsibilities of the partners. In the workplace, there are also written documents—such as job descriptions, policies and procedures, project plans—as well as specific goals and objectives that all communicate expectations between the partners.

In order for a partnership to be successful, those involved have to understand these expectations clearly. This can be difficult because not all the expectations are written down; sometimes they may not even be talked about—just assumed. For example, you may expect to *receive* positive feedback from your boss when you do something well. In turn, you *give* your boss the best work possible. However, if you don't receive regular positive feedback, you may lower the quality of your work because you think your boss fails to appreciate what you do.

The first step in developing a partnership is to understand as clearly as possible the expectations that you and your boss have for each other. The clearer the understanding, the more likely you are to have a thriving partnership that is mutually beneficial. Here are three ways you can approach the situation.

First, assume 100 percent responsibility for making the partnership work. Don't think your boss will automatically make time available for you and provide all the support you need. Don't wait for the boss to come to you, go to your boss with a plan of action. If your boss does come to you, even part way, you'll be pleasantly surprised. Waiting for that to happen can be a mistake.

Second, shoot for early successes in areas that are important to your boss. Figure out what is important to him or her and focus on getting those things accomplished. Let him or her know what you are doing and about the success you are having. When your boss realizes that you are working on the things he or she considers most important, you are more likely to develop a partnership.

Third, make a favorable impression on those your boss trusts and respects. Your success in your boss's eyes is based in part on what he or she hears from others. Make sure your interactions with the people who also interact with your boss are positive. Eventually the word will get back to your boss and be a positive force as you work to create a partnership.

Focus on Common Priorities

It is important that you and your boss work on common priorities so that you can both be successful. Although it may seem like common sense, it is not always common practice. Part of the problem is that you may think you know what your boss's priorities are and what, in turn, your priorities should be. Unless you take time to confirm what you think is true, you could be spending time and energy working on something that is not important to your boss.

In the best case scenario, you have a boss who tells you the priorities as soon as you are promoted, keeps you informed of changes, and perhaps even involves you in establishing the priorities. At the other end of the spectrum is the boss who doesn't tell you what the priorities are. This doesn't mean you have a bad boss. Your boss may just assume that you already know or because of time constraints hasn't discussed the priorities with you. Some bosses may think that the priorities are common knowledge, having been communicated previously.

If you are unsure of what the priorities are, there are ways to find out. Obviously the best way is to discuss them with your boss. Until you have the opportunity for that discussion, you may have to do a little detective work on your own. Many organizations have regular and systematic planning processes to identify vision, mission, and goals. These processes are usually documented. Ask for copies of such documents and use them to determine what the priorities are for the organization as well as within your own department.

In addition, you can do other things to get a feel for the priorities. You can read messages on the bulletin boards, in company newsletters, or annual reports, or you can obtain a copy of the company goals. When you attend meetings, listen for themes or ideas that are mentioned frequently. These can give you a clue as to the priorities. Sometimes talking to your peers provides the information you need. Since they have the same boss you do, they may be able to answer your questions. The sooner you find out what the priorities are and can start working on them, the more effective you will be in your new role.

Communicate Upward

Establishing guidelines for communication between you and your boss is also essential. Does your boss want to talk to you every day, once a week, once every two weeks, or only when time permits? Does your boss want to know about everything that happens or just about exceptions to previously developed plans? Does your boss prefer to be the one who initiates the communication or are you expected to take the initiative? Does your boss prefer e-mails, memos, phone calls, or face-to-face meetings? Regardless of the method, the most important thing is that you keep your boss informed.

You are the gatekeeper of information between your boss and your employees. You have to make decisions about what your boss tells you and what, in turn, you tell your people. Equally important is to keep your boss informed about what your people are doing. Tell you boss about their successes and how they have helped you. This provides insights into the quality of the people that you have working for you and your ability to get the most out of them. It also lets the boss know that you are building bench strength for the company. Sharing the success of your employees doesn't take away from your own accomplishments—it shows your ability as a supervisor.

Nearly every boss wants to know some specific things—your job is to communicate that information upward in the manner that the boss wants it. First, keep the boss informed on the progress of your projects. Provide updates about what has been accomplished and target dates for completing the next phase of the project. Don't be hesitant to share bad news if you are running behind schedule. It's better that your boss hears it from you than finding it out some other way.

This leads to the second important thing to communicate—anticipated problems or roadblocks. Let your boss know about these as soon as possible. Don't just state the problem—take the initiative to tell your boss what you are planning to do to solve the problem. At the same time, ask for the boss's ideas on what you could do. Take advantage of his or her experience.

Third, tell your boss when you have completed a project and ask for feedback. This shows you are getting things done and are concerned about the quality of your work. Use the feedback to guide your efforts on future projects.

Keeping your boss informed is essential to your long-term success. It is always better for your boss to get information from you rather than from someone else or through the grapevine. Always be intentional, informative, and honest in your upward communication. Keeping the information flowing upward helps your boss be successful because he has the right information on which to base decisions. Often these decisions affect you and your people, so it's important that your boss have all the information needed.

As a new supervisor, don't worry about communicating too much or too often. If you do, your boss will let you know. Think about it from your own perspective. Wouldn't you rather have too much information than not enough? Your boss is the same way. Frequent and open communication can build a foundation for developing a positive working relationship with your boss.

On the other hand, there are bosses who prefer to limit the amount of information they receive and when they receive it. Don't try to guess what the boss prefers; remember, it's up to you to take the initiative and find out. The activity at the end of this section (Exercise 2–3) provides some questions you can ask to ensure that you and your boss are both on the same page when it comes to communicating upward.

Maximize the Relationship Potential

Developing a partnership, having common priorities, and communicating upward are essential to working with your boss in a positive manner. There are several other things that you can do to maximize the relationship with your boss. First, start by ensuring you possess and exhibit the personal qualities discussed earlier in this chapter. Second, apply as much as possible of what you learn throughout this course. Third, develop good work habits and stick with them. Fourth, continually focus on what you can do to be an effective supervisor and work to improve your skills. As your effectiveness increases, so will your relationship with your boss.

Though it is always better to focus on the positive things previously mentioned, it is also important to be aware of things that you should *not* do because they can have a negative impact on the relationship. With that in mind, here are some specific things you should avoid if you want to maximize your relationship with your boss.

Don't Stay Away
It should be evident by now that you may have to take the initiative when it comes to working with your boss. Though it might seem good to be given a lot of latitude, don't be lulled into taking that as a green light to do whatever you want to do. Ask your boss for regular meetings and use that time to make sure the boss knows what you are doing, the issues you are facing, and how you are doing in meeting his or her expectations.

Don't Trash the Past or Others
Avoid pointing out mistakes that were made before you got there. Don't try to build yourself up by tearing others down. In the end, these approaches only make you look less sure of yourself. Instead, focus on what you are doing and the results you are getting. Let other people draw their own conclusions about how things are better.

Don't Embarrass Your Boss
There may be times when you are with your boss and he or she says something that you know is not exactly right. Correcting the boss publicly can have an adverse effect on your relationship. Instead, talk about the situation in private. It may be that you don't have all the information that the boss has or that something has changed that you didn't know about.

Don't Surprise Your Boss
Be willing to be the messenger who delivers the bad news. Though it may be painful, your boss would rather hear it from you than from someone else. Most bosses become more upset if they find out about problems from someone else. When that happens they wonder what you are trying to hide. Let your boss know of problems early on and ask for assistance, if needed, to get things back on track.

Don't Be Part of the Grapevine
Your boss wants someone who can be trusted with facts and won't spread rumors. When you hear gossip or rumors, tell those who are spreading them that such stories can have a detrimental affect on many people. Take steps to quash the stories and make sure you don't spread them. At the same time, don't totally discount everything you hear. Being aware of people's thoughts and feelings can help keep you informed and avoid surprises. You may want to follow up on some of the things you hear through the grapevine to verify their accuracy. Just be sure you don't pass along baseless gossip to your boss as if it were fact.

Don't Complain About the Boss to Others
If you have an issue or concern about something that your boss does, take it up with him or her. When you complain to someone else it only makes you look like someone who goes behind others' backs and can't be trusted yourself. If you are angry, confused about an assignment, or don't like something your boss said or did, always talk to your boss rather than someone else.

Don't Be Subversive

Don't attempt to get rid of your boss or have him or her fired. As previously mentioned, if you have a problem with your boss, discuss it with him or her. If that doesn't work, follow the organization's grievance policy. State your specific concerns in a clear and concise manner. Avoid suggesting that your boss should be terminated or transferred—that is not your decision to make.

Don't Be Negative

Maintain a positive attitude and approach to your job, even when it's difficult. Your negative attitude can easily rub off on others and cause them to become negative or demoralized. When a negative person comes to you, take time to address his or her concerns and get that person back in a positive frame of mind.

Don't Steal

This may seem obvious, but it covers a wide range of things. Don't steal time by not doing your work or taking extra long lunches or breaks. Put in the time and effort required and expected. Don't steal ideas or information. The things your organization does are considered proprietary—that is, they belong to the organization. Be sure you are aware of the policy on sharing information with those outside the organization. Likewise, don't steal property—paper, pens, pencils, envelopes, and the like are for your use at work, not your personal property.

✎ Exercise 3: Working with Your Boss

INSTRUCTIONS: Developing and maintaining a positive relationship with your boss requires work. Use this activity to evaluate your relationship with your boss. First, complete the portions that you can on your own. Second, arrange for a meeting with your boss to discuss your answers and/or to complete the rest of the items. Don't be hesitant to ask your boss for these answers. Though it may seem that you are being pushy, most likely your boss will appreciate the fact that you have taken the initiative to get the answers so you can work together in a positive manner.

1. Develop a Partnership
   Complete the left column of the following grid. Then meet with your boss and have him or her complete the other column.

I want from my boss a relationship that is:	My boss wants from me a relationship that is:
Each day I expect my boss to:	Each day my boss expects me to:

I will contact my boss whenever:	My boss expects me to contact him or her whenever:
The most important thing my boss can do for me is:	The most important thing I can do for my boss is:

2. Focus on Common Priorities

   The following questions help ensure that you and your boss can establish common priorities.

   What are the top three priorities for the company?

   _____

   _____

   _____

   What are the top three priorities for our department?

   _____

   _____

   _____

   What are the top three priorities for my boss?

   _____

   _____

   _____

   What are my top three priorities?

   _____

   _____

   _____

   How often are priorities to be re-evaluated?

   _____

   _____

   _____

3. Communicate Upward

   What communication method does my boss prefer to get information?

   _____
   _____
   _____

   How frequently does my boss want to get information?

   _____
   _____
   _____

   What type of things should be communicated immediately?

   _____
   _____
   _____

   Are there any things that do not need to be communicated?

   _____
   _____
   _____

   Are there any regular reports that are required? If so, is there a standardized format for the reports?

   _____
   _____
   _____

4. Maximize the Relationship Potential

   What are some things you want to be sure you do?

   _____
   _____
   _____

   What are some things you want to be sure you don't do?

   _____
   _____
   _____

© American Management Association. All rights reserved.
http://www.amanet.org/

What *Dos* are important to your boss?

What *Don'ts* are important to your boss?

FIRST-LINE SUPERVISION KEY COMPETENCIES

The first part of this chapter discussed the five roles that a first-line supervisor needs to play to ensure day-to-day success. Next, we discussed several critical personal qualities and provided a foundation for supervisory success. You also learned about the importance of developing a good working relationship with your boss. We now briefly look at the six key competencies of a first-line supervisor. Each competency consists of a bundle of skills that are used by effective first-line supervisors. Because of their critical nature, each competency is covered in greater detail in separate chapters (Chapters 3 to 8):

- Communicating
- Developing People
- Managing People
- Building a Team
- Getting the Work Done
- Supervising in a Changing Environment

All of these competencies are intertwined and several may be your focus at the same time. In other words, you can't communicate one day and develop people the next. Instead you need to use communication skills as you are developing people. The relationship among the personal qualities and competencies discussed is shown in the supervisory model in Exhibit 2–2.

Communicating

Communication is the lifeline of every organization and occurs at every level and among various levels. As a first-line supervisor, you are expected to communicate up, down, and across the organization. You will frequently be asked to communicate *up* to your boss and to those above you in the organization. You may do this through informal and formal presentations or

Exhibit 2-2
Supervisory Model

Hexagon sides (clockwise from top): Communicating, Developing People, Managing People, Building a Team, Getting the Work Done, Supervising in a Changing Environment

Personal Qualities
- Set High Personal Standards
- Be Accessible
- Inspire Success
- Accept Responsibility for Your Actions
- Emphasize Quality and Service
- Believe in Employees
- Set Priorities and Stick to Them
- Strive for Continuous Improvement

---

through written reports. You communicate *down* as you interact with those who report to you. This doesn't mean "talking down" to your employees, but simply acknowledges the fact that you have to communicate with those who are lower on the organizational ladder than you are. You also have to communicate *across* to other supervisors within the organization. Your interaction with your peers can provide you with valuable insights if you take advantage of the opportunities to communicate with them.

Successful first-line supervisors are successful communicators. In Chapter 3 you learn about the communication process, communication factors, how to make work assignments, listening, conducting meetings, written communication, and how to use communication technology to your advantage. Take time to develop these critical communication skills. With rare exceptions, you will find that those who are the most effective communicators are the most effective supervisors; they are also the ones most likely to be chosen for promotion or assignment to important positions within the organization.

© American Management Association. All rights reserved.
http://www.amanet.org/

Developing People

Your ultimate success will be judged not only by your own accomplishments, but also by the accomplishments of your people. In order to be successful, you have to help your people be successful. When they succeed, you succeed. When they fail, you fail. Your ability to develop your people will be a major factor in your ability to achieve the desired results. The most successful supervisors are those who have the best people to work with, and they have the best people because they develop their people. Effective supervisors make the most of the people who report to them.

In Chapter 4 you learn how to develop your people through three key activities: orientation, training, and coaching. Each activity focuses on providing employees with the guidance and direction they need to be successful. The better you are at helping them succeed, the better they will be at helping you succeed. It's a cycle that tends to repeat itself over and over in organizations. Effective supervisors have effective people and effective people work for effective supervisors. Conversely, look at a group that doesn't perform up to expectations and you are likely to find a supervisor whose performance is subpar.

Managing People

Two questions every supervisor asks at one time or another are: "Why do people do what they do?" and "What can I do about it?" Many first-line supervisors get frustrated when they find their people don't have the same level of motivation that they have. They often tear their hair out trying to figure out how to get people to do what they want them to do. Unfortunately, they often push when they should be pulling, or they pull when they should be pushing. Effective supervisors have learned the art of keeping their people focused so they give the best performance possible.

Some of the key topics you learn about in Chapter 5 are providing performance feedback, doing performance appraisal, working with difficult employees, managing workplace conflict, and taking disciplinary action. These and other management techniques, when properly applied, can make the difference between having a work environment where everyone gets along and works together or having an environment that puts people on edge. You learn how to set the tone for the work environment and how to keep things "humming" along.

Building a Team

Every new supervisor starts with a group of employees who report to him or her. Whether it remains a group or becomes a team depends on the supervisor. Some supervisors seem to have the knack for developing a team whereas others continually struggle to get everyone moving in the same direction. Their "knack" is really a combination of knowledge, experience, and the ability to work with a variety of people—it doesn't happen by accident.

In Chapter 6 you learn the benefits of teamwork, how to tell whether you have a group or a team working for you, how to transform your group into a team, how to be a valuable team member yourself, and how to overcome obstacles to team development. Once your team is working together and everyone is pulling in the same direction, you will find that your efforts are more effective and productive.

Getting the Work Done

In the end, it's performance that counts. What those above you in the organization expect from you are results. They want you to accomplish the goals and tasks that are within your area of responsibility. Upper management won't care if you are a great communicator, people developer, team builder, and people management expert unless you can get the job done. Never lose sight of this one important fact—if you don't get the job done, someone else will most likely be given the opportunity to see what they can do.

When it comes to obtaining top performance, you have to use all the skills described earlier. Beyond that, you also have to be effective at delegating tasks to your employees and creating a positive work environment. In Chapter 7 you learn how to plan and organize for success. Setting goals, determining priorities, and managing your time are all part of ensuring that the work that needs to be done gets done. At the end of the day, you will feel best about yourself and your team when you can honestly say to yourself, "We did it, we did it right, we did it on time, and we had fun doing it." In the end, getting the work done often becomes its own reward.

Supervising in a Changing Environment

The work of first-line supervisors has always been a challenge—even back in the days when it seemed like things remained the same and familiar routines could be followed every day. This all changed with the coming of the information age and the growing use of technology. Now with each passing day it seems that the role of the first-line supervisor becomes increasingly complex. What was true yesterday is not necessarily true today and what is true today will likely not be true tomorrow.

Chapter 8 focuses on the legal issues that you have to be aware of and be prepared to deal with on a daily basis. You learn about the impact the continually changing nature of the workforce with its increased diversity has on supervisory issues. New ways of working—virtual employees in virtual offices or distance managers supervising people at multiple and distant locations—are also addressed. The chapter concludes appropriately enough with techniques on how to manage change.

✎ Exercise 4: Strengths, Weaknesses, and Opportunities

INSTRUCTIONS: Developing your skills in each of the key competencies enables you to be a more effective supervisor. Take a moment to think about whether you consider each of these competencies a current strength, a current weakness, or an opportunity—a situation that may arise in the near future in which you can apply the competency. Circle the letter that applies and then briefly describe what action you want to take to help you build on the strengths, improve the weaknesses, or take advantage of the opportunities. Keep this sheet handy as you go through the remainder of the course.

Competency	**S**trength **W**eakness **O**pportunity	Action Required
Communicating	S W O	
Developing People	S W O	
Managing People	S W O	
Building a Team	S W O	
Getting the Work Done	S W O	
Supervising in a Changing Environment	S W O	

recap

This chapter lays the foundation for beginning to understand your roles and responsibilities as a first-line supervisor. Several important issues were discussed. First, your employees have to respect you—not the position you hold. You earn respect by demonstrating your knowledge to your employees, setting a positive example, and having the experience that enables you to be effective on a daily basis.

An effective first-line supervisor helps people by planning and organizing work, providing resources, managing and developing people, administering and controlling, and handling problems and issues.

In addition, you must posses certain personal qualities that enable you to be successful. Included are setting high personal standards, being accessible, inspiring success, accepting responsibility for your actions, emphasizing quality and service, believing in your employees, setting priorities and sticking to them, and striving for continuous improvement.

It is also important that you recognize the important role your boss plays in your success. The four keys to having a positive working relationship with your boss were discussed. First is to take the initiative to develop a partnership; second is to be sure you and your boss are focused on common priorities; third is to communicate upward in a manner that meets your boss's expectations; and fourth is to work to maximize the relationship potential.

Finally, you must develop several competencies: communicating, developing people, managing people, building a team, getting the work done, and supervising in a changing environment. The first-line supervisor who is able to integrate these roles, personal qualities, and competencies, is well on the way to success.

✎ Exercise 5: Taking It Back to the Workplace

INSTRUCTIONS: Now that you have completed the reading and the activities in this chapter, it's time to think specifically about how to apply what you have learned. The following questions are designed to help you consider what you need to do to succeed back in the workplace.

- ❑ How confident are you in your ability to perform the day-to-day supervisory roles described in this chapter?
- ❑ Have you identified any personal qualities that you need to change? If so, are you committed to making the change?
- ❑ What have you done to lay the foundation for developing a partnership with your boss?
- ❑ What do you need from your boss to be successful? Does your boss know that you have this need?
- ❑ Have you identified which key competencies you need to focus on as you complete this course?

Review Questions

1. Which of the following is *most* important to help you earn the respect of your employees?
   (a) Knowledge of the job
   (b) Job title
   (c) Job experience
   (d) Example you set on the job

   1. (a)

2. When communicating with your boss about your projects, you should:
   (a) limit the amount of information you provide.
   (b) avoid bringing up problems until after you fix them.
   (c) wait for the boss to ask about your progress.
   (d) keep the boss informed on your progress.

   2. (d)

3. What is your most important job as a first-line supervisor?
   (a) To get to know the workers and their capabilities
   (b) To get the work done
   (c) To organize your work and your workers
   (d) To check work to find mistakes and correct them

   3. (b)

4. When something goes wrong, the best thing you can do is to:
   (a) determine who caused the problem and why.
   (b) punish the person who made the mistake.
   (c) accept personal responsibility for the mistake.
   (d) use your influence to make your team look good.

   4. (c)

5. The results you achieve as a first-line supervisor depend to a large extent on:
   (a) the amount of authority your boss gives you.
   (b) the number of people you have working for you.
   (c) your own motivation and self-discipline.
   (d) your ability to survive in an environment where expectations are not always clear.

   5. (c)

3

Communicating

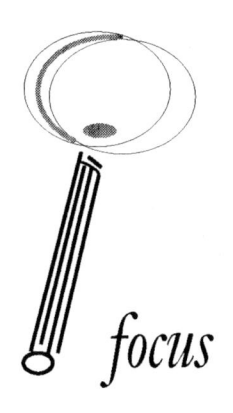

Learning Objectives

By the end of this chapter, you should be able to:

- Describe the four-part communication process.
- Identify and explain the eight factors for improving listening skills.
- Describe the steps in planning and conducting a meeting.
- Identify four guidelines for effective written communication.
- Explain how to use communication technology effectively.

"So in the final analysis, it is your effort and your effectiveness that will make you successful," Luke said as he wrapped up his presentation at the new employee orientation meeting. He received a warm round of applause and felt confident his message had gotten through. At the next break Luke talked to one of the participants. When the discussion turned to his presentation, it quickly became evident to Luke that the person had not understood his message, and so Luke tried to clarify his key points. By the time the break ended, Luke was confident the participant now understood his message. He was left wondering, however, what message the rest of the participants had heard. Had he really done a poor job of presenting or had the participant done a poor job of listening? Either way they hadn't communicated with each other.

Communication. Everyone has an opinion about it, but no one seems to do anything about it. Yet research has shown a direct connection between strong communication skills and improved productivity, a reduction in employee problems, improved working relationships, and lower turnover—

all goals of an effective first-line supervisor. It has been estimated that we spend 70 to 90 percent of every workday involved in the communication process. How we communicate with others influences the way they see us, how they react, and ultimately, the results we achieve. The best supervisors have learned the effective communication techniques explained in this chapter and apply them on the job.

Communication problems are often cited as one of the major detriments to effectiveness. Most of these problems are attributed to others: He doesn't listen. She interrupts. He doesn't understand. If only she would listen! The intimation is that, if other people would just improve their communication skills, everything would be fine. If you share this belief, you may have trouble being effective.

The best supervisors take responsibility for their own communication skills. They assume if there is a communication problem, it is because they have not made themselves clear. The best supervisors do everything in their power to maximize the effectiveness of their communication. The first step in improving communication skills is to understand the communication process.

THE COMMUNICATION PROCESS

Communication has been defined in numerous ways. Yet all the definitions have one basic feature in common—passing information from one person to another. Unfortunately, sometimes when information is passed, the end result is not what the person who passed the information expected. For communication to be successful, it has to achieve the desired results. Therefore, let's use the following as a definition of *communication:* "passing information from one person to another with the intention of getting a specific result."

Exhibit 3–1 shows how the definition looks when it is put into practice. The key word in the definition is *specific*. Most of our communication gets results of some kind. We ask someone to do something, and they do it. We may find out later, however, that what they did was not exactly what we had in mind. The result is called a *communication problem* because we didn't get the specific results we wanted. A breakdown in communication can occur at any point in the process. By examining each part of the process, we may be able

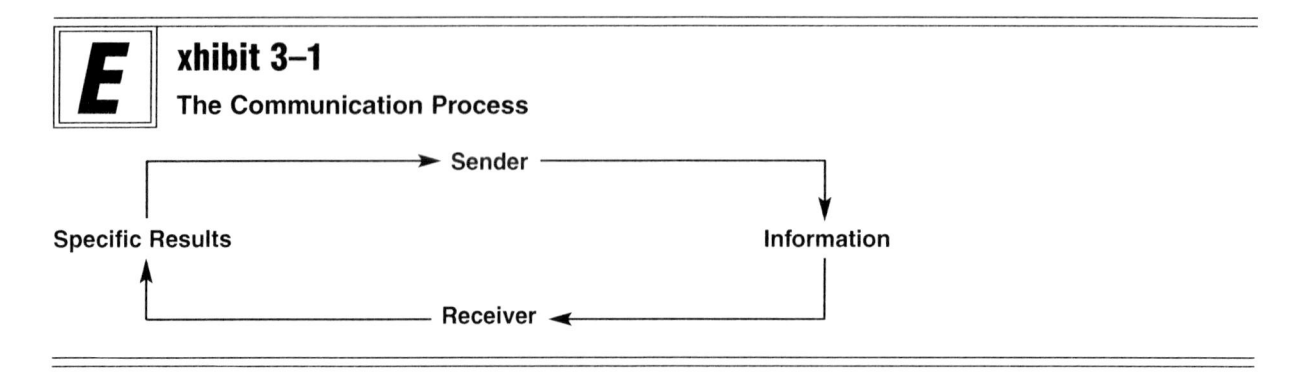

Exhibit 3–1
The Communication Process

Specific Results → Sender → Information → Receiver → Specific Results to determine the cause of a communication breakdown. Here's how the four-part process works:

1. The *sender* has information that starts out as a thought. The sender puts that thought into words or symbols and sends the information.
2. The *information* is either fact or opinion. It may come in the form of a question, a statement, a request, an instruction, or an order.
3. The *receiver* takes the information and "translates" it into his or her own thoughts. The success of the sender, at this point, may depend on how well the receiver translates the information.
4. The *specific results* ultimately depend on how the receiver regards the message and the sender.

The sender knows the information was received properly if the specific results that were expected actually occur. If the results are different from those intended, the communication was not successful.

As mentioned earlier, effective supervisors take responsibility for the success (or failure) of their communication. This willingness to take responsibility is one characteristic that separates effective supervisors from those who are ineffective. Therefore, rather than placing blame or finding fault with an employee, the effective supervisor first assumes that the problem was with the information sent, not with the employee receiving it.

Effective supervisors make sure they know what they want before they try to communicate it to someone else. They make sure those receiving the message are ready for it, and they let them know that questions should be asked if they don't understand.

Effective supervisors also take responsibility for the success of communication when they are the ones receiving it. In other words, they make sure they understand the message someone is sending them. Have you (receiver) ever received an assignment (information) from your boss (sender) and completed it (result) only to find out that it wasn't what the boss wanted (specific results)? Taking responsibility for communication means making sure you understand the information you receive. It may take a little work, but in the long run you'll save time and energy if you help your senders clarify their messages so you can deliver the specific results they expect.

If you don't understand what you are supposed to do, ask questions. The adage, "The only dumb question is the one not asked," certainly applies when you are the receiver of communication. If you make a habit of asking clarifying questions, after a while you will find that those who are sending you messages become more effective communicators, because they will anticipate your questions before they send you a message.

✎ Exercise 1: Communication Breakdowns

INSTRUCTIONS: Read each of the following situations and then indicate which part(s) of the communication process broke down.

1. Xavier is the shift supervisor at "Always Pressed for Time" dry cleaners. A customer recently dropped off three sweaters for dry cleaning and

Xavier took the order. The customer didn't mention anything special about any of the sweaters and Xavier passed them on to his employees for cleaning. Now, Xavier is checking the work done by one of his employees and notices that all the sweaters have been "cleaned," but that there is a stain on the sleeve of one of the sweaters. The customer was told the sweaters would be ready at 3:00 P.M. today and its now 2:30 P.M.

___ Sender ___ Information ___ Receiver ___ Specific Results

2. Sandra supervises the day shift at a local clothing retailer. Earlier today she walked into the break room and found it a mess. At the end of the shift, she told the employees that the break room was a "mess and needed to be cleaned" before they left for the day. Thirty minutes later they all left and said the break room was clean. When Sandra checked a few minutes later, the room was better, but it still wasn't up to her standards.

___ Sender ___ Information ___ Receiver ___ Specific Results

3. Marques asked Genny to provide a complete report about a project she's been working on for several days. When Marques received the report he discovered that it didn't contain all the information he expected. He couldn't understand why Genny gave him such an incomplete report.

___ Sender ___ Information ___ Receiver ___ Specific Results

4. Helen supervises a team of accountants. Her boss, Ricardo, asked her to change several accounting procedures. Ricardo told Helen that the suggestions came from department managers and vendors. Helen heard Ricardo describe the need to simplify the budgeting process and find a faster way to process accounts payable. Helen worked with her team and made the changes she thought Ricardo wanted. When she presented them to Ricardo, his response was, "That's a good start, Helen, but you need to go further than that." Helen was disappointed and resentful that the work she and her team did was not appreciated. As she left Ricardo's office she thought to herself, "I can't ever please him. He always asks for more!"

___ Sender ___ Information ___ Receiver ___ Specific Results

Suggested Answers
Situation 1: The sender failed to give Xavier complete information. However, Xavier (receiver) has to accept responsibility for how the communication was received. He should have been proactive and asked the customer if there were any special cleaning problems so the cleaning could have been done properly.

Situation 2: Sandra's (sender) communication was too general. Saying the break room was a "mess" was based on her definition of a mess. She should have been more specific about what she wanted cleaned up—such as tables, the floor, cabinets, etc.—so employees would know the standards for a clean break room.

Situation 3: Marques's communication got results (a report), but not the specific results (complete information) he wanted. The communication breakdown occurred because Marques didn't specify exactly what he wanted in the report, or because he assumed Genny would know what to put in the report. By the time Genny redoes the report, it will most likely take more time than if Marques had clearly explained what he wanted when requesting the report.

Situation 4: Helen (receiver) should have been more proactive when Ricardo was explaining the assignment. Helen needed to do a better job of clarifying Ricardo's expectations so that what she presented was in alignment with what he wanted. By relying on her assumptions of what Ricardo wanted, Helen spent unnecessary time and effort working on the wrong thing.

? Think About It

Think about a recent communication breakdown you have experienced. Take a moment to describe what happened for each part of the process; then determine where and why the breakdown occurred.

Sender: _____
Information:

_____
_____
_____

Receiver: _____
Specific Results:

_____
_____
_____

Where did the breakdown occur and why?

_____
_____
_____

LISTENER PROBLEMS AND SOLUTIONS

Everyone has horror stories about listening—or the lack of it. The body is present, but the mind has left the room. It has been estimated that we only remember about 20 percent of what we hear. Primarily this is because in most listening situations the listener is only paying attention part of the time. Successful supervisors are aware not only of the message they are trying to get across, but they are also aware of the fact that people have trouble listening.

People may be bored, distracted by personal problems, concerned about something that is about to happen or has just happened, or a hundred other things. The one thing you can be sure of is that they aren't giving you 100 percent of their attention. With a little luck, they may mentally return and check out what you're saying once in a while. Sometimes, once lost, they never come back. Have you ever daydreamed through sermons, meetings, or classes in school? If so, you know how hard it can be to pay attention—even when you know it's in your best interest to do so.

As a supervisor, it is your responsibility to hold the attention of your employees when you are speaking—whether it's one-on-one or in a group situation. Your success in gaining and holding their attention depends on how well you organize what you are saying. Organize your communication, express a willingness to accept and give feedback, and use appropriate visual materials to support your message.

Your listeners may not ask you the following questions, but they are thinking of them, and unless each question is addressed, your chances for successful communication are reduced.

What Is This All About?

What is the subject being discussed? Get to the point as soon as possible. This is one reason why an agenda is so important, even for the smallest and shortest meeting. An agenda puts things in proper order. If listeners have to wait or search for the reason for the message, their attention will be lost.

Exactly What Is Being Proposed?

Make clear what you are proposing and the specific results you expect. If it is not made clear, there is usually confusion about the intended results. If a decision is being made, this is the time to explain the reasons, and what is involved. When people understand and accept a proposal, they listen more attentively. Unless the subject is covered carefully, people may leave the discussion feeling that time has been wasted and nothing accomplished.

Why Is It Needed and by Whom?

If listeners don't believe they need what is being proposed, it will be difficult, maybe impossible, to get them to act either as individuals or as a group. Explain why it is important and to whom. Identify who is involved. Be prepared to answer questions to clarify what you want.

Exhibit 3-2
Presenting Ideas to Match Listener Needs

Subject: State clearly what the discussion is about.
Proposal: Clearly define the proposal.
Need: Explain why it's important, and to whom.
Benefit: Validate the potential benefits.
Action: Define the action or decision to be made.

What's in It for Me?

Most of us are constantly tuned to station WII-FM: What's in it for me? When speaking, don't generalize; be as specific as possible. Identify how the group or individual will benefit from what you are proposing. Validate what is being proposed in the form of data, the experience of others in similar situations, analogies, or some form of expert outside advice. Use all the tools at your disposal to communicate benefits.

What Is Supposed to Be Done About It?

This is the place to establish who is responsible for what. If there are reports to be submitted, identify who will do the work and to whom they report. If there are assignments or deadlines, each person involved should indicate an understanding of his or her role in what has been decided. This is when you must especially take care to be specific (see Exhibit 3–2).

Even when all of these concerns have been addressed, many people still have a tendency to criticize new ideas. If there is reluctance to act, you have an obligation to sell the group on the benefits of what you are proposing. By describing practical applications for a group, suggesting useful ideas, and pointing out the value of certain actions, you have a better chance to overcome objections.

Think About It . . .

Think about a specific idea you currently need to communicate to your employees. Take a moment to describe what you can do to proactively address potential listener problems.

What Is This All About?

_____

_____

_____

Exactly What Is Being Proposed?

_____

_____

_____

Why Is It Needed and by Whom?

_____

_____

_____

What's in It for Me?

_____

_____

_____

What Is Supposed to Be Done About It?

_____

_____

_____

_____

IMPROVING PERSONAL LISTENING HABITS

Most people think that the speaker is totally responsible for the content of the message, but the listener has an equal responsibility to pay attention, provide sincere feedback, avoid critical judgments, and avoid self-imposed distractions. When there are discussions, meetings, or presentations, there is usually an exchange of ideas; thus your own listening skills are important. Having a reputation for being a good listener and making a serious effort to understand what's being discussed can improve your chances for success. Here are eight steps you can take to improve your personal listening habits:

1. Listen for ideas, emotions, and feelings.
2. Listen for what is *not* being said.
3. Control your emotional reactions.
4. Overcome personal prejudgments and distractions.
5. Keep an open mind.
6. Listen more than you talk.

7. Hear the other person out (don't interrupt).
8. Use open-ended questions for active listening.

Listen for Ideas, Emotions, and Feelings

Most of us tend to listen for the facts and pay less attention to theories and conceptual ideas. However, even the poorest communicator can be the source of an idea. You can usually learn something by listening intently in every situation. Sometimes the person speaking may not have all the facts, so listen for concepts and ideas.

You also need to listen for emotions and feelings to pick up vital informational cues that are not stated, but are important to know. For example, does the speaker's voice sound urgent, enthusiastic, reserved, or cautious? You need to listen for these verbal cues to emotions and feelings so that you can fully comprehend everything being communicated.

Listen for What Is Not Being Said

We often assume we know what the other person means or what he or she is going to say before it's said. We may seem to be listening, but we don't really hear what is being said. We put our words (instead of theirs) in their mind and miss the intent of the message. Then we respond with what we thought they were going to say instead of what was actually said.

Likewise, it's important to pay attention to the responses you get from your employees. Their responses tell you whether they are listening to you. For example, you may give an employee an assignment and get a simple response of "Okay." Is it really "okay" or is the employee just saying that without really listening? Look for clues such as the lack of eye contact, the quickness of the reply, the "let's get on with it" attitude. All could be signs of not listening accurately.

Control Your Emotional Reactions

Sometimes you must appropriately assert yourself, and being a supervisor means that you will be involved in emotional issues. However, keep the lid on any over-emotional reactions.

Ignore the other person's attire, awkwardness, language, biases, mannerisms, or habits. For example, a person who is dressed in a manner that you consider unacceptable, makes a comment about a subject being discussed. However, because of the way the person is dressed, you may be inclined to make up your mind ahead of time that whatever the person says won't have much merit.

Avoid bringing up emotional side issues in group situations. A discussion or meeting is seldom the place to allow or create emotional reactions. Questions or comments that irritate or intimidate can backfire. People tend to remember the incident and forget the issues or logic involved. If other people ask hostile or emotional questions, keep calm and get the subject back on track. If you have to disagree with what is being said, do so in as positive a manner as possible.

© American Management Association. All rights reserved.
http://www.amanet.org/

Overcome Personal Prejudgments and Distractions

Poor body language can reveal inattention or indicate indifference to an aware speaker. Stay alert and pay attention. This may not be easy after a long lunch or during a busy day, but it is important. In addition, avoid dismissing the other person's ideas as something already known or heard before. The person may have something additional to contribute.

Keep an Open Mind

Few people admit to having anything other than an open mind, but the truth is somewhat different. Too often, people fail to listen carefully because they are "expecting" something. Avoid tuning out the other person. Listen for something you can use; it's probably there.

Listen More Than You Talk

You can listen much faster than you can talk. The average person listens at 500 words per minute, but only speaks at about 125 words per minute. Use this extra time to your advantage to make sense of what is being said. It isn't essential that the message be enjoyed; just be sure it is understood. When you have grasped the message, acknowledge your understanding to the speaker.

Hear the Other Person Out (Don't Interrupt)

Pay attention and be sure to understand what is going on. Many people interrupt because they perceive the subject as uninteresting, or they feel they have something to add. Interrupting tells others that we are not truly listening. By developing the ability to listen without interrupting, you can pick up a great deal of useful information that otherwise would be missed.

To avoid missing critical material, save any pertinent questions or comments until the other person is finished. Listening without interrupting is particularly helpful in situations where changes are occurring or in handling disagreements. Someone may be throwing curves, and an interruption may let them get away with it.

Use Open-Ended Questions for Active Listening

Open-ended questions are those that cannot be answered by a simple yes or no. To encourage meaningful communication, avoid doing all the talking and ask questions frequently. Open-ended questions allow others to express how they feel or to explain some point more clearly. Open-ended questions usually begin with words or phrases such as *who, what, when, where, why, how,* or *tell me about that.* Using active listening implies more than merely hearing the other person out. The following examples of active listening do not cover all the possibilities, but they provide some useful guidelines.

Check Whether You Have Been Understood
Questions at this point let you check to see whether you are "on track." The magic words to remember are *feel, felt,* and *found:*

> "How do you feel about what I've said so far?"
> "I wanted to find out how you felt about this."
> "Have you found this idea will work?"

Note that it's easy to reply to a question about feelings. If there is an objection or some problem, you have an opportunity to acknowledge it and answer it immediately.

Check Whether You Have Understood the Speaker
There are times when the speaker has not covered the subject clearly or adequately. Regardless of how well you listened, you may need more information. Rather than pointing out their omissions or mistakes, rephrase the statement and then ask a question: "Let me see if I understand what you just said. As I understand it . . . (rephrase the statement). However . . . (bring up the point you want explained)."

In some cases, the speaker may make a number of points, but not all are clear to you. The process is similar. Rephrase the speaker's comments but summarize the specific issues you want clarified. "Let's review what you've said so far. As I heard you, you said . . . (rephrase and then close with the question:) Is that correct?"

Improving your listening skills is one of the best ways to ensure your success as a supervisor and possibly open up future opportunities for yourself elsewhere within your organization.

✎ Exercise 2: Active Listening

INSTRUCTIONS: The following activity takes twenty to thirty minutes to complete effectively and requires one or two other people. You may want to schedule a specific time to complete it later. Use this activity to help you develop your ability to practice active listening. The activity works best with three people: a Speaker, a Listener, and an Observer. However, you can do it with one other person by combining the Listener and Observer roles. If possible, ask some of your peers to do the activity with you so you can all work on developing your skills.

When you are ready, have the Speaker talk to the Listener for two to three minutes about some topic. The more controversial the topic, the better, since this challenges the listener to use active listening skills. Some topics to consider are:

- Capital Punishment
- Legalized Drugs
- Government Spending
- Violence on Television
- Gun Control

After the Speaker is finished, the Observer (or Observer/Listener) gives feedback to the Listener based on the following questions. After a brief discussion, change roles and repeat the exercise. Repeat as often as necessary until you are comfortable that you are able to practice active listening.

Did the Listener:

Yes	No	Listen for ideas; not just facts?
Yes	No	Control emotional reactions?
Yes	No	Overcome personal judgments?
Yes	No	Keep an open mind?
Yes	No	Listen without interrupting?
Yes	No	Use open-ended questions to clarify understanding?
Yes	No	Restate the message accurately?

Comments/Suggestions

_____

_____

_____

PLANNING AND CONDUCTING MEETINGS

When Michelle was promoted to first-line supervisor she decided the best way to get things started would be to hold a meeting with her employees. She reserved a room and communicated the time and place to everyone. She made a few notes and was ready when everyone arrived. Once the meeting started Michelle quickly covered the key points she had written down. She asked if anyone had any questions and no one said anything. Michelle looked at her watch and realized they had only been there for ten minutes even though she had planned for a one-hour meeting. Since she didn't have anything else to say and no one had questions, she dismissed the meeting. She knew people liked short meetings, but she also knew that she had not accomplished much in the short time they were together. Michelle realized that she would have to do some more work prior to her next meeting.

One of the ways in which you will likely do a lot of communicating with your employees is during meetings. First, accept the fact that meetings are a time to get important work done. In today's workplace, people spend more and more time in meetings. Your challenge, like Michelle's, is to make them productive and ensure they achieve the intended results.

As a rule, you want to have a meeting when it is the most effective and efficient way to share information or make decisions. Keeping this rule in mind helps you avoid the problem of too many or too few meetings.

The fact is that properly conducted meetings save time—lots of time. Meetings save time because everyone gets the message at the same time. When everyone gets the message at the same time, questions can then be asked and issues clarified, and everything does not have to be repeated for each individual.

In addition, grapevine gossip is reduced. Communications that have to be passed on from worker to worker are often subject to individual interpretation. The specific outcome you intended by your communication may get lost in the process. Having the entire group present can minimize misunderstandings as well as save time. Deadlines, priorities, and responsibilities can be settled without repetition when everyone is operating from the same page.

Preparing an Agenda

For maximum efficiency, even the smallest meeting should have an agenda. Providing a list of subjects to be covered helps people listen specifically for pertinent information. Agendas also prevent meetings from degenerating into discussions of side issues or becoming gripe sessions.

Developing an agenda is important because it forces you to prepare for the meeting. Preparation is the key to a successful meeting. The time you spend thinking about the meeting in advance should help save you time during the meeting. Exhibit 3–3 lists basic questions that should be considered for every meeting. Answering these questions ahead of time helps you keep focused. The answers may also lead you to conclude that you aren't

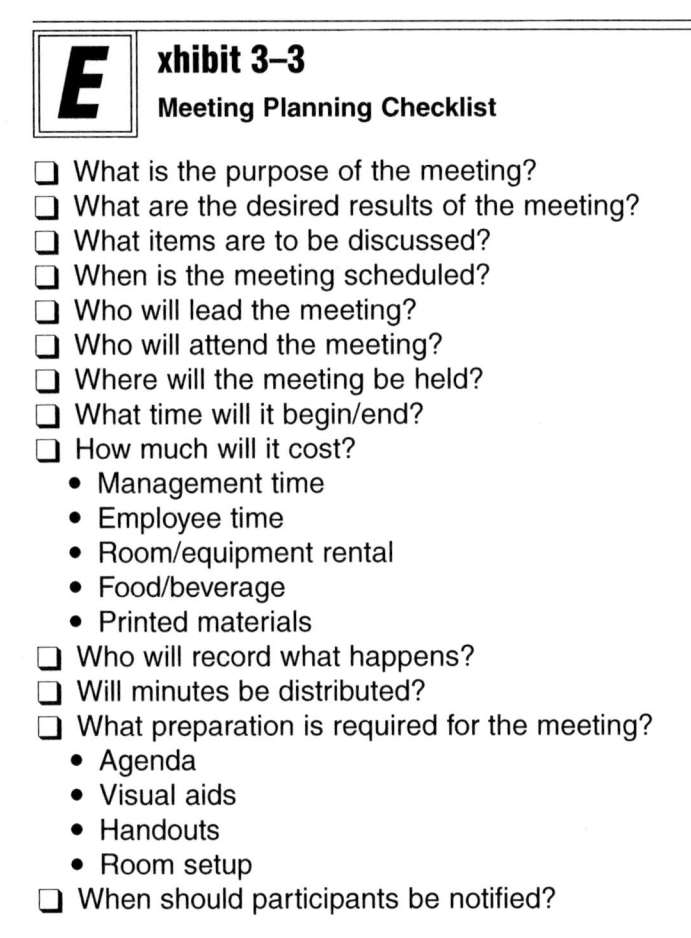

Exhibit 3–3
Meeting Planning Checklist

- ❏ What is the purpose of the meeting?
- ❏ What are the desired results of the meeting?
- ❏ What items are to be discussed?
- ❏ When is the meeting scheduled?
- ❏ Who will lead the meeting?
- ❏ Who will attend the meeting?
- ❏ Where will the meeting be held?
- ❏ What time will it begin/end?
- ❏ How much will it cost?
  - Management time
  - Employee time
  - Room/equipment rental
  - Food/beverage
  - Printed materials
- ❏ Who will record what happens?
- ❏ Will minutes be distributed?
- ❏ What preparation is required for the meeting?
  - Agenda
  - Visual aids
  - Handouts
  - Room setup
- ❏ When should participants be notified?

ready for a meeting right now because you don't have all the information you need.

Whenever possible, the meeting agenda should be distributed ahead of time so participants have time to think about the items and come prepared to discuss them. If that's not possible or practical, have the agenda on the table when people arrive for the meeting. This gives them a chance at least to get a feel for what will be covered. At the beginning of the meeting, take a few minutes to briefly review the agenda. This sets the tone for the meeting and clears up any questions participants might have about its purpose.

Use Exhibit 3–3 as a checklist when planning future meetings.

Conducting the Meeting

Conducting a meeting is much easier with a prepared agenda. You have a control tool in front of you and all the participants. If things start to get out of control or people get off the subject, you can always refer back to the agenda to regain control. Begin the meeting by reviewing the agenda and stating approximately how much time you expect to spend on each item.

Present the information the group needs to know. Also offer information the group wants to know. This is one way to prune the grapevine. When people are kept informed through regular, consistent meetings that dispense the information they need, the grapevine becomes less relevant and less disruptive.

Allow time for group discussion and questions. Respond as honestly as possible and keep the group focused on the subject at hand. Pay attention to the mood of the group and learn to "read" their body language. If you notice people getting restless or losing interest, take a short break. Watch out for the one-on-one discussions that sometimes develop between meeting leaders and one or two participants. These discussions can quickly turn off other participants. Control these situations by inviting these individuals to talk to you about their concerns after the meeting.

Use the "parking lot" technique to capture important topics that may come up, but are not related to the agenda. Simply write the words "Parking Lot" at the top of a flip chart and post it where everyone can see it. Then when a non-agenda item comes up it can be "parked" for later rather than taking up valuable meeting time. Make sure before the meeting is over that some decision has been made about how and when the parking lot items will be addressed. Otherwise it just looks like you are trying to avoid the topic.

Assign someone to record any decisions that are made and any responsibilities that are assigned. This serves four purposes: First, it lets participants know that you are serious about what's being discussed at the meeting. Second, it gives you a way to follow up on specific assignments. Third, you can use the information to close the meeting. Fourth, if you wish, you can send meeting minutes to participants after the meeting.

Close the meeting by summarizing the key decisions and responsibilities. Let people know what you expect and when you expect it. This is your chance to ensure that your communication will obtain the specific results you intend.

Exhibit 3-4
Meeting Evaluation

I would like your feedback about our last meeting. Circle your answer to the following questions and then return the survey to my attention.

Meeting Topic _____ Date/Time _____

Yes	No	Did you receive an agenda?
Yes	No	Did the meeting accomplish the stated purpose?
Yes	No	Did the meeting stay on schedule?
Yes	No	Was there enough time allowed for the meeting?
Yes	No	Was everyone present who needed to be there?
Yes	No	Was a record kept of what was agreed to?
Yes	No	Was the audiovisual support appropriate?
Yes	No	Were the necessary printed materials available?
Yes	No	Was the meeting environment acceptable?
Yes	No	Was a clear list of assignments made at the meeting?
Yes	No	Is another meeting needed? If so, when will it be scheduled?
Yes	No	Were minutes distributed within forty-eight hours of the meeting?

Comments/Suggestions

_____

_____

_____

After the Meeting

Once the meeting is over, decide whether you will provide minutes of the meeting. If so, do it as soon as possible, preferably within forty-eight hours after the meeting. Prepare the minutes while the meeting is still fresh in your mind as well as the minds of the participants.

It is also important to evaluate your meetings to ensure they are effective. You should regularly solicit feedback from those who attend. Then use the feedback as a way to improve your future meetings. Exhibit 3-4 can be used as a meeting evaluation tool.

Brainstorming

Depending on the purpose of your meetings, from time to time you may want to use a technique called brainstorming. Brainstorming is a method of leading a discussion that encourages involvement. When conducting a brainstorming session, be sure to have plenty of paper. If possible, use a large chart pad that everyone can see. Have plenty of markers so once the session

© American Management Association. All rights reserved.
http://www.amanet.org/

begins you can quickly write down everyone's ideas. As you fill one page, start a new one. Save all pages for reference later.

Follow these rules when conducting your brainstorming session:

- *Withhold negative criticism of ideas.* Do not stop to discuss any ideas for any reason. Do not allow anyone in the group to criticize an idea or say something like, "We've tried that before." Your goal is to get as many ideas as possible.
- *Encourage freewheeling.* Anything goes in a brainstorming session. No idea is too wild or far-fetched. Remember you are trying to come up with ideas that are new and different.
- *Go for quantity.* Keep the group going so that ideas feed off each other. The more ideas, the better. This is one time when quality is not as important as quantity. You will refine the ideas later when you discuss the ideas that have been generated.
- *Combine ideas and make them better.* This is the last step, but don't do it too soon. Let the group think. Be willing to have some "silent time" during the session. Often the best ideas occur after there has been some silent time to think. Once you think you have all the ideas, start discussing them. Try to combine ideas and look for ways to make improvements in what has been suggested.

You probably won't want or need to use brainstorming at every meeting you conduct. Nevertheless, it is a technique you should learn to use as it can help generate new ideas and novel ways to solve problems.

WRITTEN COMMUNICATION

Meetings are valuable because they allow you to communicate a lot of information to a group and agree jointly on plans or actions. As a first-line supervisor you also need to use a variety of written communications, such as written reports and memos. Writing that is unclear, vague, or poorly organized leads to mistakes, misunderstandings, and confusion, and it wastes time. Think back to our discussion of the communication process at the beginning of this chapter. Our definition of communication—"passing information from one person to another with the intention of getting a specific result"—certainly applies to written communication.

The late Groucho Marx used to tell the joke about how he was hunting in Africa and got up one morning and shot an elephant in his pajamas. Then he said, "How he got in my pajamas, I'll never know." Through the use of a few misplaced words, the meaning of what he was saying got changed. This sometimes happens to us when we aren't careful about the way we approach our written communication.

Think about the reason you are writing a memo. Do you have something important to say that will be received in a positive manner? How many times have you received a memo and become angry about what it said? How many times did it create a "downer" day for you? Did you ever think, "Why didn't he just tell us in person?" Unfortunately, many memos are written by ineffective supervisors who are "hiding" from their employees. They are afraid to face them directly and often put things in writing that they would never say in person. The result is a negative experience for the person who receives it.

Effective communicators prefer face-to-face communicate over written communication. For many people written communication is more difficult than spoken communication because you can't see or hear the person to whom you are writing. You can't see facial expressions, the person can't ask you questions, and you can't ask questions to determine whether the other person understands. All of these factors make it likely that your message may be misinterpreted or misunderstood by those who read it. Therefore, it is important that if you decide to use written communication that you take steps to make it as effective as possible. Here are four guidelines you can apply when preparing written communication.

Organize Before You Write

If you plan to take a trip to some place you haven't been before, you would use a map to provide directions. The same is true of writing. If you want to wind up at your destination (to achieve specific results), you need to have a road map. When writing, an outline is your road map. Use a two-step approach to develop your outline. First, briefly write down all the ideas and pieces of information you want to include in your written communication. Second, organize the ideas into an outline with major headings and sub-points. These two simple steps help you get rid of extraneous material and focus on your objective.

Use Simple, Straightforward Language

Strive for clear communication. Avoid buzzwords or slang. Keep sentences short. Complicated sentences and unusual phrases only confuse the reader. Memos should be no longer than one page. Anything longer and the receiver is likely to get tired of reading—and not get your message.

Be Sensitive to the Tone of Your Writing

Avoid writing when angry. If the message is critical, it may be wise to have someone else read it before you send it. Avoid exclamation marks to drive home a point!!!! They look out of place in business correspondence and give the impression that you can't control feelings. AVOID USING ALL CAPS LIKE THIS WHEN WRITING AS IT MAKES THINGS HARDER TO READ BECAUSE THE INDIVIDUAL WORDS AND LETTERS TEND TO RUN TOGETHER AND BECOME HARD TO DISTINGUISH FROM ONE ANOTHER.

Write from the Viewpoint of the Reader

Readers pay a great deal more attention to a message when it is written with their interests in mind. If you are writing to correct a mistake, write from the other person's point of view. Remember, your reader is tuned to WII-FM (What's In It For Me). Define how the person will benefit, rather than what the consequences will be if the conduct is not changed. Whenever possible, have someone else read your communication before you send it. That person can tell you whether your message will be accurately received and may also be able to offer suggestions for improvement.

Exercise 3: Evaluate Your Written Communication

INSTRUCTIONS: Go through your files and retrieve your last three pieces of written correspondence. Answer Yes or No based on the preceding guidelines. If necessary, indicate how it could have been improved.

Written Communication #1: _____

Yes   No   Was it necessary or would some other method have been better?
Yes   No   Was it organized?
Yes   No   Was the language simple and straightforward?
Yes   No   Was the tone correct?
Yes   No   Was it written from the reader's viewpoint?
How could it have been improved?

_____

_____

Written Communication #2: _____

Yes   No   Was it necessary or would some other method have been better?
Yes   No   Was it organized?
Yes   No   Was the language simple and straightforward?
Yes   No   Was the tone correct?
Yes   No   Was it written from the reader's viewpoint?
How could it have been improved?

_____

_____

Written Communication #3: _____

Yes   No   Was it necessary or would some other method have been better?
Yes   No   Was it organized?
Yes   No   Was the language simple and straightforward?
Yes   No   Was the tone correct?
Yes   No   Was it written from the reader's viewpoint?
How could it have been improved?

_____

_____

COMMUNICATION TECHNOLOGY

In today's business world, technology has provided us with multiple and ever-evolving methods designed to improve our ability to communicate. Unfortunately, technology alone does not automatically improve communication, and poor communication skills are not enhanced with new technology. In fact, the opposite is often true. Those who generally communicate poorly in written form now just do it more often because of the easy access to more ways to communicate. Likewise, poor verbal communicators may send out more messages that are hard to decipher because they can simply pick up the phone and send a message.

Electronic communication has many advantages. One significant advantage is that text messaging, instant messaging, and video and telephone conferences provide more opportunities for two-way communication. They also reduce the time frame for responses and can save wasted meeting time by allowing people to communicate from wherever they are rather than bringing them all to one place.

However, be aware that there are situations in which face-to-face communication is best, such as very sensitive issues. The same is true for complex issues that require a series of decisions by several people. When seeking major commitments, face-to-face discussion is more effective, especially if you have to make a case for things like more resources or more budget dollars. Similarly, when you need to consider several possible solutions to a problem, or when people have multiple perspectives, a meeting of all parties is often a quicker way to get resolution.

The guidelines just presented in the Written Communication section also apply when using the various forms of communication technology. Remember to (1) organize before you write or talk; (2) use simple, straightforward language; (3) be sensitive to the tone of your writing or speech; and (4) write or speak from the viewpoint of the receiver of your communication.

This section briefly discusses guidelines for using some of the more common methods of communication technology. It is not intended to be an exhaustive list, but rather a cross-section of available technologies.

Electronic Messaging

Through e-mail, text messaging, and instant messaging, you most likely get more communication from other people than ever before. One person can easily and quickly send a message to twenty other people by pressing a couple of buttons or clicking a mouse. The ease of using electronic messaging has made it the mode of choice for written communication. Don't confuse quantity with quality. It is important that when you use these technologies to communicate with others that you do so in an appropriate manner.

Think of your electronic messages as you would any written communication. Use an electronic message only if you would put the same thing on paper where anyone could see it and read it. Don't send a message that defames or slanders another person or organization. Your e-mail or other messages could wind up in a court of law as evidence against you or your company—it has happened to major corporations. Protect yourself and your company by using electronic messages only for normal, day-to-day communication. Avoid the controversial or opinionated message that someone else could misinterpret.

Even though electronic messaging is quick and easy, your thought process should be reflective and sound. For example, comments that are even slightly suggestive in nature might be interpreted as sexual harassment by the receiver—even though you meant nothing of the kind. Likewise, a message sent as a reprimand could be misunderstood by the receiver. Any type of personnel issue is best dealt with using two-way communication where you can see and hear the response of the other person.

Avoid using electronic messages to communicate confidential information. The possibility exists that someone other than the intended recipient may open and read a message. Also, some people automatically print out all their messages and then read them later. When the receiver prints it, someone else may pick it up off the printer and read what you have written. Confidential information is best communicated in writing and placed in a sealed envelope, or handled in a face-to-face meeting.

Always remember that one-way communication can easily be misinterpreted by the reader. You can't see the recipient's face or reaction to what you have written. Use electronic messaging for its intended purpose—to enhance productivity.

Your electronic messages are a reflection of you. If you want to have a professional image, your messages should reflect that. Make sure they are necessary and sent only to those who need to receive them. Use a style and tone that conveys your seriousness and professionalism. The best way to maintain a professional approach is to follow one simple rule—don't put anything in your electronic messages that you wouldn't say to someone face-to-face.

Voice Mail

Like electronic messaging, voice mail can create problems if not used appropriately. Some people use voice mail as a way to avoid face-to-face contact. Some people use voice mail because they don't know how to use electronic messages. Some even use voice mail as a way to blow off steam.

Don't say anything that might be misinterpreted by the person listening to your message. Most voice mail systems allow the receiver to save a message. When using voice mail, think of what you are saying as "the whole truth, nothing but the truth." It may be tempting to say something on voice mail that you would never say to someone's face—especially when they can't immediately respond to what you have said. Make sure that you don't say something in your voice mails that you might regret later.

Some people use the speakerphone feature when listening to messages. You may send a message to someone in confidence, but it may wind up being heard, even accidentally, by someone else. For this reason, when receiving voice mail, avoid using the speakerphone unless you have an office where you can shut the door so others can't overhear your messages.

Avoid saying anything in a voice mail that is intended to be confidential and that you wouldn't want someone else to hear. Don't use voice mail to send a message that you would be embarrassed or concerned if someone other than the person for whom the message was intended, heard your message. Save your confidential messages for face-to-face meetings or closed-door meetings.

Use appropriate language when sending voice mails. Off-color words or statements should never be used. Don't say anything that could embarrass you, the listener, or someone who might overhear your message. Only say in a voice mail what you would be willing to put in writing for someone to see, read, and re-read. Say what you have to say succinctly and clearly. Get to the point and keep your message brief. It's not necessary to repeat your message—if the receiver wants to hear it again, he most likely can replay it.

Always keep in mind that your voice mail is a reflection of you. Your voice mails should be clear, straightforward, and easy to understand. Use your voice mail to provide information. Deal with controversial or personnel-type issues only in face-to-face meetings.

Internet or Intranet

The Internet is a source of a wealth of information. Many people rely on it to do research, check facts, and keep up on the latest information about virtually any topic. Many organizations also make use of the Internet or their own organization's intranet for employee training and development. As with other technologies, the key is the manner in which it is used.

First, don't waste your time or your company's time surfing the Net or looking up things for your own personal use on company time. Make sure you are using your company time for legitimate work-related purposes. It can be easy to think, "I'll take just a minute to check on something" while you are online and wind up spending lots of minutes doing something that is not work-related. Some organizations keep logs of how their employees use the Internet as a way to monitor and discourage inappropriate use.

Second, try to verify the accuracy of the information by checking more than one Web site as well as other sources of information. Just because something appears on the Internet doesn't make it true. There are lots of tabloid-type sites that stretch the truth or make up their own versions of the truth. There are really no restrictions on who can say what on the Internet. That doesn't mean that all the information is bogus, but it does mean "surfer beware." Therefore, think before you automatically use something you find.

Third, remember that you are a role model for your people. Effective supervisors make effective use of their time and expect the same of their people. If you spend time surfing when you should be working, you'll have trouble keeping your people from doing the same.

Conferencing

Conferencing via video, telephone, and Web sites can save organizations time and money when there is a need to get several people together. Often these conferences can be arranged in a short period of time and help keep the organization moving forward. Everything you learned in this chapter about having a meeting can be applied to conferencing. Here are a few keys to remember.

First, have an agenda and communicate it ahead of time. You may want to give others the chance to add to the agenda or you may have a specific agenda you want to follow. Either way, having an agenda in front of everyone helps keep the conference on track.

Second, give participants a chance to identify and introduce themselves if they don't already know each other. This helps establish credibility and rapport before the conference gets started. It also allows people to get used to the technology so they speak at an appropriate level and look in the right direction.

Third, follow up with minutes of the meeting. Capture the key decisions that were made and who is responsible for those decisions. As with a regular meeting, a forty-eight-hour turnaround is preferable while the meeting is still fresh in everyone's mind.

Cellular Technology

Cell phones, camera phones, and pagers seem to have become as necessary as a six-shooter was to the old-time cowboy. In fact, the number of people with holsters for their technology weapons sometimes makes it look like a technology fight could break out at any minute. Though these devices certainly have increased the frequency of communication, there hasn't been a corresponding improvement in quality. Here are a few things to keep in mind when using these technologies.

First, be courteous and respectful to those around you. Turn these devices off or to vibrate when attending meetings so you don't cause a distraction or disturbance. If you have to talk to someone, leave the room and handle the call in private—no one else needs (or wants) to hear your conversation. Avoid taking calls when in a one-on-one meeting unless you want to convey to the person with whom you are meeting that he or she is "less important than the person who just called me."

Second, maintain confidentiality. If you have a camera phone, don't take pictures on the job of things that might be considered proprietary unless you have permission. Don't take pictures of people in unflattering situations. Avoid discussing things that may be confidential in the presence of others. Keep in mind that a person who hears only half the conversation can easily misinterpret the real message.

Third, practice safe use. Many organizations now have policies against cellular use while driving company vehicles or while on company business. They understand the safety and liability issues that could arise if an accident occurs and its cause can be traced to inattention due to a cellular device.

Computer Systems

The laptop computer, file sharing, and database management are just a few examples of the proliferation of communication options that are available. Laptop computers along with easy Internet access make it possible for people to be "connected" to other people and their work 24/7. For some this is a distinct advantage, while others view it as a real negative. Regardless of your view, here are some things to remember.

First, establish protocols and standards for such things as file sharing where several people have access to and the ability to change files. It is important for system integrity that everyone understand the rules of use and that they abide by them. Otherwise, the system is ripe for both unintentional misuse and intentional abuse.

Second, be clear in your expectations for how your employees should use these systems. What should they do and not do? How often should they "check in" electronically? How can they use these tools to improve productivity and work quality?

In all likelihood, communication technologies will continue to grow at an ever-faster pace. Do your best to keep current on the changes and use them in a way that enables you and your people to be more effective without becoming a slave to the technology.

Exercise 4: Communication Technology

INSTRUCTIONS: Are you using communication technology in an appropriate manner? Take a moment to evaluate how you use various methods and whether you need to change what you do in order to use your technology more appropriately.

Method	Currently used for:	What other method (including face-to-face) could be used:
Electronic Messaging		
Voice Mail		
Internet or Intranet		
Conferencing		
Cellular Technology		
Computer Systems		
Other		
Other		

What improvements can you make in using communication technology?

_____

_____

_____

recap

In this chapter, we discussed the importance of communication and how it can determine your success as a first-line supervisor. We emphasized making sure your communication achieves the specific results you intend and on taking responsibility for the success of your communication.

Your role as a first-line supervisor requires that you spend time listening to others. In this chapter, you were given eight ways to improve your listening habits. Listen for ideas, not just facts; listen for what is not being said; control your emotional reactions; overcome personal prejudgments and distractions; keep an open mind; listen more than you talk; hear the other person out; and use open-ended questions for active listening.

This chapter also provided you with guidelines for planning and conducting meetings. When handled properly, meetings and group discussions can be valuable communication tools. You read about how to conduct brainstorming sessions to generate new ideas and solve problems.

Finally, the chapter addressed issues around written communication and communication technologies. You were given four guidelines for effective writing that you can use when writing memos or reports. You also learned some guidelines when using electronic messaging, voice mail, Internet and intranet, conferencing, cellular technology, and computer systems.

Exercise 5: Taking It Back to the Workplace

INSTRUCTIONS: Now that you have completed the reading and the activities in this chapter, it's time to think specifically about how to apply what you have learned. The following questions are designed to help you consider what you need to do to succeed back in the workplace.

- ❑ Do you need to improve your listening skills? If so, what is your plan for doing so?
- ❑ How would you rate the effectiveness of your meetings? How could they be improved?
- ❑ How effective is your written communication in achieving the intended results?
- ❑ Have you discussed and agreed upon the appropriate uses of communication technologies with your employees?

Review Questions

1. The communication process consists of the following parts: 1. (d)
   (a) sender, receiver, facts, and message.
   (b) sender, receiver, and information.
   (c) sender, receiver, message, and information.
   (d) sender, receiver, information, and results.

2. When using electronic messages, you should: 2. (c)
   (a) use abbreviations to help convey your true feelings.
   (b) respond immediately to messages you receive.
   (c) be aware that your message could be misinterpreted.
   (d) use them to replace most face-to-face communication.

3. It has been estimated that we only remember _____ of what we hear unless we work at listening. 3. (b)
   (a) 10 percent
   (b) 20 percent
   (c) 30 percent
   (d) 40 percent

4. A meeting agenda is important because it: 4. (a)
   (a) gives the person conducting the meeting more control.
   (b) encourages a free flow of ideas and topics.
   (c) forces people to listen instead of trying to take over the meeting.
   (d) leads to a longer, more thorough meeting to discuss pertinent topics.

5. Brainstorming is a method of communication that encourages: 5. (b)
   (a) employee restraint.
   (b) employee involvement.
   (c) better listening.
   (d) evaluation of ideas.

4

Developing People

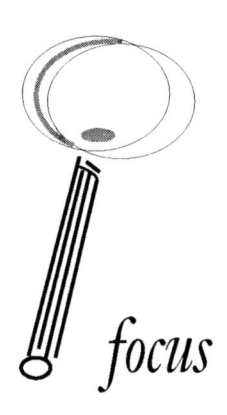

Learning Objectives

By the end of this chapter, you should be able to:

- Explain the steps involved in developing people.
- Develop and use a new employee orientation plan.
- Develop and use an employee training plan.
- Explain how to ensure training is effective.
- Coach employees to improve their performance.

Steven Reinemund, CEO of PepsiCo, was cited by *Business Week* (January 10, 2005) as one of the best managers because of his ability to develop people as well as products. The article pointed out how he takes a major role in mentoring and teaching employees and expects other senior managers to do the same. The result is a strong leadership bench that helps PepsiCo tap new markets. Though you may not yet be a CEO, as a first-line supervisor you do have responsibility for developing your people.

PEOPLE DEVELOPMENT

Let's begin with an overview of some of the benefits of developing people along with the types of development activities and procedures you can use.

Benefits

When your people are successful, you'll be successful, because your success is tied directly to the people working for you. Having good people also enables you to be more effective and efficient, because your people are able to accomplish more with less of your time and involvement.

You may have people working for you who have the potential to move up in the organization, or they may have the potential to work in other areas of the organization. In some cases, they may not need or want to change jobs, but they have the potential to improve their current job performance. When you help them, you also help your organization benefit by having more fully developed people.

Types of Development Activities

As the supervisor, your development activities begin as soon as employees are hired and they continue as you work with them on a daily basis. This chapter focuses on three specific people development processes over which you have control:

1. New employee orientation
2. Employee training
3. Coaching employees

When you take the time and make the effort to develop your people and help them be successful, it will, in turn, help *you* be successful.

Setting Goals and Maintaining Focus

The demands and pressures of your day-to-day responsibilities can make it difficult to find the time to develop your people. You simply have to invest the time and energy to make it happen. The emphasis you place on these development activities will be paid back several times over by having employees who contribute more and do so sooner than if you expect them to develop themselves.

Although there is no easy solution to the problem, one thing that helps is to develop plans and set goals that help you maintain your focus. For example, you should have a definite plan for when and how you will conduct new employee orientation. Some suggestions are provided later in this chapter. Having a plan and then sticking to it can go a long way to ensuring you are successful in developing your people. The same applies for employee training and coaching.

You can also maintain a top-of-mind awareness of the importance of developing people. Look for opportunities to develop your people each day. Training does not always have to be a formal process. For example, when you are working with an employee who is having a problem completing a specific task, you can provide some on-the-spot training that will help him or her at that moment and also will benefit in the future. Such teachable moments likely occur on a regular basis—you just have to be alert for when they happen and then take advantage of the opportunity that presents itself.

NEW EMPLOYEE ORIENTATION

What happens to an employee the first few days on the job can have a significant impact on his or her long-term success. Getting off to a good start makes everything else easier. A bad first day or week may have a negative impact that prevents employees from reaching their full potential. In fact, according to Judith Stevens-Long and Michael L. Commons in their book, *Adult Life: Developmental Processes*, 50 to 60 percent of employees leave their jobs after only seven months of employment.

One reason people leave their jobs is that they never feel welcome or part of their work group. As a result, they soon begin looking for another place to work and become a turnover statistic. For the first-line supervisor, this statistic may mean more work for those who are still on the job, lower productivity, and lower morale.

A well-planned orientation program can reduce turnover and save an organization thousands of dollars. Whether an organization has two employees or 20,000, an effective new employee orientation program pays for itself in a short period of time.

Most employees arrive for work on the first day full of enthusiasm and excitement as well as anxiety and uncertainty. The initial interest employees show can either be put to positive use or be dampened, depending on first impressions and experiences. The goal of orientation is to capitalize on each new employee's enthusiasm and keep it alive once the work begins. When orientation is successful, the new employee is more likely to become a valuable asset to the organization.

Objectives

An effective new employee orientation program accomplishes the following objectives:

- Provides a welcome
- Develops positive perceptions about the organization
- Confirms the employee's decision to join the organization
- Sets the stage for training
- Puts the employee at ease

Provide a Welcome

You never get a second chance to make a good first impression. Orientation is the time to roll out the red carpet and let employees know you're glad they joined the organization. Many organizations have elaborate going-away parties for employees when they leave, but do nothing special when they start to work. This sends a not-so-subtle message that leaving is a cause for celebration. Here are some ways you can provide a welcome to new employees:

- Set aside the first two hours of the day to spend with the new employee.
- Have a welcoming party.
- Put the employee's name and picture in the company newsletter.
- Put the employee's name and picture in the local newspaper.

- Buy the employee's lunch the first day.
- Assign another employee to be available to answer questions during the first week on the job.

Develop Positive Perceptions

During orientation, employees develop perceptions about the organization and the people who work there. Their perceptions of you as their boss are greatly influenced by what you do and don't do during those first few days. A planned and organized orientation communicates that you are in control and that the organization cares about its employees.

New employees are aware of the work environment. They notice how well things are organized and whether a business-like atmosphere exists, and they soon decide whether this is an enjoyable place to work. This initial opinion, once formed, can be hard to change. Everything that happens during the first few days—both good and bad—is reported to friends and family. For these reasons, the quality of the orientation is a reflection of the quality of the organization.

Confirm the Employee's Decision

The orientation should allow employees to confirm that they made the right decision in coming to work for you and your organization. In many cases, employees who are hired have applied for other positions as well. If you thought they were a good choice, other organizations probably felt the same way. A new employee may have received more than one offer but decided your organization was the best place to work. What happens during the orientation should reinforce the employee's decision to come to work for you.

How many times do new employees leave an organization a few days or weeks after starting to work? It's not uncommon. Usually the reason is, "This wasn't what I expected." You greatly decrease the chances of this happening by having an organized method for orienting new employees.

Set the Stage for Training

Orientation is the time to get employees started on the right foot. A thoughtful orientation should answer most basic questions new employees have. When these questions are answered, the employee can focus attention on learning the new job.

If you don't have a well-planned orientation program, employees are forced to learn on their own. This is not only time consuming but also inefficient, since employees don't always get all the information they need. When given proper direction, a clear assignment, and specific information, new employees are more likely to be receptive when their training begins.

Put Employee at Ease

The first day on the job is filled with anxiety and uncertainty for most new employees. Almost all want to make a good first impression and do things right. In their effort to make a good impression, some may do things that seem out of place to you. Others may hold back and do little, if anything, until told what to do.

One of the best ways to put new employees at ease is to introduce them to their new co-workers in a friendly and relaxed manner. The sooner new employees get to know their co-workers, the more they feel like a part of the team. Once they feel accepted, they are more likely to be productive and happy in their new jobs.

✎ Exercise 1: Kamile's Orientation

INSTRUCTIONS: Kamile showed up for work bright and early on her first day. After a few introductions and a cup of coffee, her new boss, Javier, told her to go to a nearby office supply store and pick out a desk and some supplies. The only other thing he told her was to have it completed by two o'clock. He didn't even tell her how much she could spend.

She found the store, picked out a desk and a few supplies, and asked for same-day delivery. By two o'clock the desk was in place and she was beginning to get her supplies organized. A little later Javier stopped by to see what she had picked out and how she was doing. He told her she was off to a good start and he would see her tomorrow.

Although this scenario may seem far-fetched, it actually happened—only the names have been changed. In fact, Kamile became a long-term and valued employee at the company. Many new employees faced with a similar first day assignment would not have been as resourceful. The ambiguity of the assignment would have led them to frustration or even leaving and never returning to work.

If you had been in Kamile's place, what would your reaction have been?

_____

_____

What would you have liked Javier to do on your first day?

_____

_____

Developing an Orientation Plan

Each new employee is different and has different abilities. Your orientation is more effective when you take these differences into account. Let the employee have some control over the amount of information covered and the sequence in which it is covered. Ask new employees what they want to learn first and use this information to formulate a specific plan.

At the same time, it is important that you have a standardized list of items to cover with new employees. The Orientation Checklist in Exhibit 4–1 provides a list of the most common items that should be covered during an orientation. Use this list as a starting point when you are ready to develop a list specifically for your organization.

Exhibit 4–1
Orientation Checklist

The following are common items that should be covered during new employee orientation. The items are listed in four categories; you may wish to arrange them differently. What is important is having a comprehensive list and covering every item. Use the space provided to add your ideas.

Administrative

- ___ Employment application   ___   _____
- ___ Employment benefits   ___   _____
- ___ W-4 form   ___   _____
- ___ Noncompete agreement   ___   _____
- ___ Insurance forms   ___   _____

Personal

- ___ Work area   ___   _____
- ___ Building tour   ___   _____
- ___ Introduction to co-workers ___   _____
- ___ Parking   ___   _____
- ___ Time off   ___   _____
- ___ Vacations/holidays   ___   _____
- ___ Dress/appearance/uniforms ___   _____
- ___ Mail   ___   _____
- ___ Probation period   ___   _____
- ___ Sick pay   ___   _____
- ___ Telephone procedures   ___   _____
- ___ Employee discounts   ___   _____
- ___ Personal use of equipment ___   _____

Business

- ___ Job description   ___   _____
- ___ Organization chart   ___   _____

Exhibit continued on next page

© American Management Association. All rights reserved.
http://www.amanet.org/

Exhibit 4–1 continued from previous page

___ Hours/work schedule ___ _____

___ Pay rate/pay days ___ _____

___ Incentive pay ___ _____

___ Operations manuals ___ _____

___ Company policy ___ _____

___ Confidentiality ___ _____

___ Company history ___ _____

___ Office supplies ___ _____

___ Company publications ___ _____

___ Employee handbook ___ _____

___ ID card ___ _____

Miscellaneous

___ Recreation activities ___ _____

___ Local items of interest ___ _____

Having a prepared orientation checklist when you sit down with new employees on the first day goes a long way toward meeting the objectives described earlier. When they see you are organized, they are more likely to feel good about their decision and have positive perceptions about the organization.

Conducting New Employee Orientation

When you conduct new employee orientation, try to make the first day memorable in a positive way. Get things started correctly and the rest of the orientation will go much smoother. A common mistake is to try and cram everything into the first day. Think of orientation as a process, not a one-day event. Schedule the orientation over several days so new employees have time to digest all the information. Remember, new employees are nervous the first day, and they may have trouble remembering everything if you try to cover too much.

Once the new employees' starting date has been confirmed, make sure you are available that day to get them started. Be there to greet them when they arrive and do everything you can to make them feel welcome. As the supervisor, it is your responsibility to get the ball rolling. You may delegate some portions of the orientation, but don't delegate the first few hours. This is your opportunity to set expectations and help get your employees in the right frame of mind for the job.

Many supervisors make the mistake of not giving new employees a real work assignment on the first day. Instead of being given something meaningful to do, they spend the day reading policy and procedure manuals, quickly becoming bored with the whole orientation. Remember, new employees are eager to demonstrate the skills you hired them to perform. Wise supervisors take advantage of this situation and get their new employees to work as soon as possible.

Another critical time is the lunch break on the first day. Make every attempt, at least on the first day, not to leave the employees alone at lunch time. If you cannot be present, be sure someone in your group is available and responsible for taking the employees to lunch. If possible, buy the employees' lunch on the first day.

The way the first day ends is just as important as the way it begins. On the way home, as new employees reflect on the day, their last impressions are likely to be the strongest. Therefore, before the first day ends, spend a few minutes talking to your new employees. Find out what they are thinking. Ask them questions about their experience and how they feel about it. Let them know you appreciate their efforts and look forward to seeing them again the next day. End on a positive note, the same way you do when a guest leaves your house. Walk the employee to the door and do your best to make a good parting impression.

Remember, orientation is a process, not a one-day event. Spread things out over several days and schedule a variety of activities to keep new employees involved and interested. Allow time for information to slowly soak in rather than drenching new employees with information all at once.

EMPLOYEE TRAINING

As a first-line supervisor, you will frequently need to train new employees or provide retraining to existing employees. Training is important to an organization and should be looked at as an investment. Getting a satisfactory return on that investment can only be achieved when training is properly planned and executed.

Benefits of Training

Effective training benefits both the organization and its employees. These benefits can be very real to an organization through increased productivity, greater customer satisfaction, and better quality products. Employees also benefit from training through improved job satisfaction, greater peer acceptance, higher self-esteem, increased opportunity to advance in the organization, and higher earning power.

Use the four-step training method presented in the next section to train employees to develop the skills needed to be successful in their jobs. When employees are successful, you realize the benefits.

Failure to Train

Unfortunately some first-line supervisors and their organizations fail to train their employees properly. Untrained employees can give a negative image to the organization and cause it to lose customers, which means lost sales and profit dollars. You can probably think of retail outlets you *used* to patronize, but something happened and you said, "Never again!" Not only has that outlet lost your business, but you've probably also told several other people about your experience and encouraged them to shop elsewhere.

As a first-line supervisor it's up to you to invest the time and money necessary to train your employees. As one executive put it, "If you think training is expensive, try ignorance." How many dollars in sales or profits can you afford to lose because of untrained employees?

Identifying Training Needs

Before you do any training, it is important to determine whether there is really a need for training. Training is used to change behavior, increase knowledge, or develop skills. One way to determine whether training is needed is to ask the question, "Could he do it if his life depended on it?" If you can answer "yes" to that question, then the person already has the knowledge and skills to do the job and training is not needed. If the answer is "no," then training is one of the ways to improve performance.

The best way to answer the preceding question is to observe the employee doing the job. If, during the observation, you see things being done that are not correct, discuss them with the employee. Your discussion can help you determine what behaviors need to be changed, what he or she does or does not know, or the skills he or she does or does not have. Then you can focus your training on the specific behaviors, knowledge, or skill that needs to be improved.

Keep in mind that with new employees you almost always have to provide training so they can do the job the way you want it done. You may hire someone who has the basic skills to do the job, but you still have to train the person to do it the way your organization wants. If, after employees have worked for a while and you notice that their performance does not meet standards, then you need to determine if they need training. In some cases, they may just need some simple reminders or a little bit of coaching (discussed later in this chapter) to get their performance back on track.

Four-Step Training Method

The four-step training method was developed by the U.S. military during World War II and was used to train thousands of troops. This method, with very minor modifications, has since been used in numerous industrial, retail, and office training situations. Once you understand how it works, you can apply it to meet your training needs.

There are many advantages to using the four-step method:

- *It's easy to use.* Though it does require some planning and organization, it's not complicated.

- *You can train on the job.* You don't need a classroom or a lot of expensive equipment. You can do the training anywhere it's needed.
- *You don't have to be a training expert.* The only requirements are that the person doing the training has to want to train, have adequate job knowledge, and be able to apply some basic training principles.
- *It's easy to develop.* Every training outline follows the same four steps: (1) preparation, (2) presentation and demonstration, (3) tryout, and (4) follow-up.

Let's examine each step in more detail. As you read about each step, have Exhibit 4–2 nearby and fill in the blanks to develop your own training plan for a specific topic on which you need to train your employees.

Step 1: Preparation
The preparation step sets the stage for the steps that follow. Proper preparation makes the rest of the training easier to execute. Effective preparation also makes it easier for employees to learn more quickly. You need to prepare four things:

- Yourself
- The Training Materials
- The Place
- The Employees

Take a moment now to complete the Preparation section of Exhibit 4–2. As you do, think about some specific training that you are expected to do on a regular basis with your employees.

Step 2: Presentation/Demonstration
This is the "show and tell" step. During this portion of the training, you utilize an outline or a checklist to ensure you cover all the relevant information necessary to perform the job.

The outline you develop should be as detailed as necessary so you don't forget to cover some pertinent information. If you plan to delegate the training to someone else, your outline may need to be somewhat more detailed than one you would use yourself. The outline should be organized in the order you want to present the material. Don't forget the second part of this step demonstration. You can't just present information; you also have to show the person what you want them to do. In most cases, you show and tell simultaneously so the employees connect what you're saying with what you expect them to do.

When demonstrating a task, slow down so the employees can see exactly what you're doing. Explain that once they learn the job, you'll expect it to be done at a faster speed. Then demonstrate how fast you want the job done so they know what the standards are. Allow new employees to start slower at first. Once they learn the job, they will pick up speed.

Take a moment to continue developing your training plan by completing the Presentation and Demonstration section of Exhibit 4–2.

Exhibit 4–2
Four-Step Training Planner

Step 1: Preparation
    A. Objectives (what the employees should be able to do)

_____

_____

    B. Materials and equipment

_____

_____

    C. Prepare the place

_____

_____

    D. Prepare the employees

_____

_____

Step 2: Presentation and Demonstration
Develop your outline below. Use a separate outline for each of your training objectives.

_____

_____

_____

_____

_____

_____

_____

Exhibit continued on next page

© American Management Association. All rights reserved.
http://www.amanet.org/

Exhibit 4–2 continued from previous page

_____
_____
_____
_____
_____
_____

Step 3: Tryout
I will have the employee practice the following tasks as I observe:

_____
_____
_____
_____
_____

During the tryout I will:

- Have employee explain the task
- Correct mistakes in a positive manner
- Give positive feedback when job is correct
- Allow employee to practice at his/her own pace
- Be patient
- Back away and let employee practice alone

Step 4: Follow-Up
If the employee has questions or problems, he/she should go to:_____
_____
For this particular task I will check back every _____ hour(s) for _____ days.
Based on my follow-up, I will check back in the future every _____ hour(s) for _____ days.
No additional follow-up required:_____

Evaluation Results:
  Employee suggestions:_____
_____
_____
_____

  Changes I want to make:_____
_____

© American Management Association. All rights reserved.
http://www.amanet.org/

Step 3: Tryout

Tryout is often overlooked when conducting training because the trainer assumes that once the presentation and demonstration have occurred, the employee should be able to do the job. However, the only way to confirm the employee's ability is to give him or her a tryout while the trainer observes. During the tryout, the trainer has the opportunity to clarify any misunderstandings the employee may have and correct any mistakes. Equally important, the trainer can provide positive feedback to let the person know the job is being performed correctly.

Continue developing your training plan by completing the Tryout section of Exhibit 4–2.

Step 4: Follow-Up

Follow-up is the last step. Normally your follow-up happens at a time different from the first three steps. After the tryout is completed, you should back away and allow the employee to work alone. After a period of time, observe the employee again, providing encouragement and correcting mistakes. This follow-up may be repeated over the course of hours, days, or even weeks, depending on the job being learned. It is imperative that you follow up often enough so the employee does not develop bad habits.

You can do several things to make your follow-up more effective:

- *Have the employees work alone.* You can build confidence by letting them know that you think they are ready to do the job without your help.
- *Designate someone to go to for help.* Someone needs to be available to answer questions or help with problems that may occur. In most cases, this is you, if you did the training. However, there may be other people who can help out too.
- *Follow up frequently.* Follow up often at first, gradually backing away as you gain confidence in the employee's ability.
- *Ask questions to ensure understanding.* By asking questions, you can find out just how much the employee knows. Use open-ended questions so the employee has to give you more than just a yes or no response.
- *Do an evaluation.* Evaluate your training approach. Ask the employee what changes, if any, could be recommended to improve the training in the future. Do your own evaluation. It may uncover problems in one or more of the four steps. If you find problems, make changes before you do the training again.

Take a moment to continue developing your training plan by completing the Follow-Up section of Exhibit 4–2.

Being an Effective Trainer

Damien was the new supervisor of customer service. He had been rated as one of the company's best customer service representatives before he was promoted. Shortly after his promotion he hired two new employees, Sasha and Kendra, to be customer service representatives. He decided that they would begin their first day with a couple of hours of new employee orientation and a couple of hours observing experienced customer service representatives. Then after lunch, he would begin their formal training. Damien put together an outline following the four-step training method. After explaining the procedures for handling customer complaints, he had them do a role-play with Sasha being the customer and Kendra being the customer service representative. It didn't go very well so he had them switch roles and do it again. The second time seemed worse than the first.

Damien decided they weren't paying close enough attention so he repeated the training on the procedures and had them do the role play again, but it wasn't much better. Frustrated, he made the comment, "This isn't rocket science. If you can't figure it out I'll have to hire someone else. I was able to learn it the first day when I started to work here. I'll give you one more chance. Let's see if you can get it right this time." Unfortunately for everyone involved, the situation got worse as Damien lost his patience and cancelled the training. The next day Kendra did not show up for work. Although Damien was well respected for his customer service skills, his first experience as a trainer did not go as he hoped. What Damien didn't realize was that there is more to being a trainer than simply being good at a particular task.

The four-step training plan is a valuable tool, but using it successfully requires that you practice a few basic training principles to make you an effective trainer. The skills necessary to be an effective trainer are both similar to, and different from, the skills necessary to be a first-line supervisor. Just as being good at a particular task won't make you good at supervising that task; the best workers are not always the best trainers. Effective trainers possess certain skills and qualities. The combination of these skills and qualities as well as the use of the four-step training method helps you be an effective trainer.

Good Communication Skills
Communication used during training has to produce specific results, as we discussed in Chapter 3. The communication skills of listening, taking responsibility for your communication, and providing clear direction are all important for the successful trainer.

Knowledge and Experience
The best trainers know their subject forward and backward. They have firsthand experience in what works and what doesn't. They know how to get the job done quickly and efficiently.

Patience
Patience is the quality that most often separates successful from unsuccessful trainers. It's also the reason why the best performers are not necessarily the best trainers. Some people don't have the patience to work with someone who is new and makes mistakes. These people expect everyone to learn the job and get on with it. Their lack of patience can frustrate the person who is trying to learn a new skill and can't master it fast enough to meet the demands of the trainer.

Interest in Training

If you don't like training in the first place, you probably won't be very good at it. Some people like the idea of helping someone learn a new skill; they enjoy teaching others. If you enjoy what you do, you are much more likely to be successful at it.

Respect of Peers

How do the other employees view the person doing the training? Do they respect that person's knowledge and experience? If not, they may make comments to the person being trained that undermine the efforts of the assigned trainer. The best trainers are recognized by their peers as good at what they do and qualified to train others.

Sense of Humor

Things can go wrong during training. Mistakes are bound to happen. You may see things you've never seen before as employees are learning their jobs. As long as no one gets hurt, everything will be okay. Sometimes the best way to handle mistakes is to laugh—not *at* the employees, but *with* them.

✎ Exercise 2: Rate Your Qualities as a Trainer

INSTRUCTIONS: Rate yourself on each of the qualities of an effective trainer. Use the scale of 1 to 10 (with 1 being "poor" and 10 being "excellent").

_____ Communication Skills

_____ Knowledge and Experience

_____ Patience

_____ Interest in Training

_____ Respect for Peers

_____ Sense of Humor

Action Plan

Look at any item that you rated as less than a 7. What do you need to do to be an effective trainer?

_____

_____

_____

_____

Making Sure Training Is Effective

Cal recently returned from a one-day training session on time management that his supervisor, Marcia, had recommended. Marcia had read the training brochure closely and the content seemed to cover all the right things for Cal. Marcia was hoping to see some improvement in the way Cal used his time and the way he determined what he should be working on each day. As she talked to him and worked with him, it became apparent that his work habits had not really changed. He was the same old Cal doing the same old things. Marcia wondered why Cal's training hadn't stuck with him.

Making sure that training is effective—or to put it another way, making sure training sticks—is another responsibility of first-line supervisors. This is true whether it is training that you conduct yourself, training that someone else in the organization conducts, or training at an outside seminar such as the time management session Cal attended. Though you may never be able to make training stick 100 percent, you can do some things to make the training experience more effective and to get value for the training dollars invested.

Have a Pre-Training Meeting

Perhaps the most important thing you can do is to meet with the person prior to the training and talk about expectations. Find out what the person expects to learn during the training and what he will do differently after the training. Share your own expectations as well. Then make a written list of objectives for the training that you both agree on. Some supervisors take this a step further and develop a training contract that both parties sign and date. If that makes sense for you and your organization, by all means do it.

At the least, make sure the expectations are written down. This simple act of taking time to talk to the person communicates that you consider the training important. When you write it down, it reinforces the importance of the training. The written list also serves as a reminder for the employee of what things to pay attention to during the training.

Have a Post-Training Meeting

The post-training meeting should occur as soon as possible after the training is completed and while it is still fresh in the employee's mind. Just having the meeting reinforces with the employee the importance you place on the training. Even if you do nothing more than ask a couple of questions, your interest lets the employee know that you are serious. If you really want to have an impact, the meeting should be more specific. First, get out the list the two of you made prior to the training. Go over it and determine what items were covered. Modify the list if necessary until you have both agreed on what new behaviors and skills the employee will use as a result of the training. At this point you should have an agreement on what the employee will be doing on the job.

Provide an Opportunity to Perform

We are all familiar with the phrase, "Use it or lose it." Think of all the things you have learned over the years (such as algebra for me) but can no longer do because you haven't used the skills for some time. Sometimes the same thing happens in our workplace. People get sent for training, but then they aren't given the opportunity to use what they have learned. For example, an employee attends a project management seminar, but then is assigned to work on the project rather than manage it. Or a person attends a class on how to be an effective trainer, but then doesn't train anyone for several months. By the time he finally gets to try out his new training skills, the person has forgotten much of what was learned. Before you send someone for training, make sure they will have an opportunity to use what they learn when they get back. The less time between the actual training and when the person tries out the new skills, the better.

Ensure a Supportive Environment

The work environment can be a big plus or minus when it comes to making training stick. It only takes one or two "I don't care what you learned in training, we don't do it that way here" comments to slow down or even stop the most determined employee. Most people don't like to swim upstream, which is what they have to do when they get criticized for trying to use their new skills. Do everything you can to make sure the rest of the people will be just as supportive of the employee as you are. Also be aware of potential obstacles in the environment that can have a negative impact on trying to use new skills. Some examples include not having the right tools, not having enough time, not having the right resources, having different priorities, and working with unrealistic deadlines. You can probably think of many more. As a supervisor you need to identify the obstacles and get rid of them as best you can.

Encourage and Recognize Improvements

Everything will not go perfectly the first time employees try out new skills. Encouraging them to try again and to recognize the improvements they have made can lessen the impact of any mistakes. Let them know that you know they are working hard. Let them know that you can see the progress.

Everything you have done up to this point will be all for naught if you don't continually provide feedback and recognize the accomplishments that have been made as a result of the training. People tend to keep doing things when they receive positive feedback for doing them. If you want training to stick, you have to let them know that you recognize the changes they have made as a result.

✎ Exercise 3: Making Training Stick

INSTRUCTIONS: Take a moment to think about some upcoming training that either you are doing for your employees or that they will be attending. What will you do to help make the training stick?

- Describe the when, where, and what of your pre-training meeting.
  _____
  _____

- When will you have your post-training meeting?
  _____
  _____

- What will you do to ensure the employees have the opportunity to perform?
  _____
  _____

- What will you do to ensure a supportive environment?
  _____
  _____

- What will you do to encourage and recognize improvements?
  _____
  _____

COACHING EMPLOYEES

Coaching is not just telling employees what to do and then sitting back and expecting them to do it. Coaching, like orientation and training, is another way of helping people achieve their full potential. Jeffrey H. Davis (1995) defines workplace coaching as "working directly with an employee to improve a specific job related skill or behavior, or even overall performance." Coaching success, he points out, depends on recognizing those employees who are (and who are not) candidates for coaching and then evaluating the factors that affect your decision to coach.

Key Factors in Assessing a Possible Coaching Situation

Davis says there are three factors to consider when choosing a coaching situation:

1. How significant is the performance area in furthering your department's mission?
2. How much time do you have to give to the coaching project?
3. How coachable is (are) the person(s) involved?

The Significance Factor
Not every performance issue that occurs in the workplace is significant enough to warrant coaching. As a first-line supervisor you have to decide

just how important the problem is to your team's success. Problems that are most likely to need your attention as a coach are those that involve the bottom line, productivity, significant use of time and resources, accuracy or error rates, setting priorities, or employee discipline. If you decide the problem is not worth pursuing, you have to work around it to minimize its effect. You may even have to learn to live with it. On the other hand, if you determine the problem is significant you should use the coaching process to resolve the situation.

The Time Factor

The time factor tells you when to pursue the coaching opportunity. Once you have determined the problem is significant enough to warrant your attention, you have to decide when to schedule the coaching discussion. Coaching is not something you do in a five-minute conversation as you pass an employee in the hall. The more difficult or serious the situation, the longer it is likely to take. The coaching process may begin with a forty-five minute meeting and then continue on with a series of shorter meetings.

Your job as a coach consists of helping other people solve their own problems, rather than simply providing solutions. This can take time. You have to be willing to listen while the other person identifies solutions to a problem. If you do all the talking, you are not coaching; you are simply telling people what to do. The coaching process takes time when it is done right, but it can lead to positive coaching results.

The Coachability Factor

Some employees are more amenable to coaching than others. Some people are looking for help and welcome coaching intervention. Others may be reluctant or even downright resistant to your coaching efforts. Since coaching is a one-on-one activity, you have to learn to adapt your approach to the employee. Just as the situational leadership styles discussed in Chapter 1 indicate the importance of choosing a style that fits the employee, the same thing holds true for coaching. If you don't approach employees in a way that they will be receptive, your coaching efforts likely will not yield the results you want.

Determining the coachability factor of an employee can be subjective. However, don't shortchange your employees. Some people are more open to help than they may appear to be. If they know you are sincere in wanting to help them, they may be more receptive to your coaching than you think.

✎ Exercise 4: To Coach or Not to Coach?

INSTRUCTIONS: Read each of the following situations and indicate whether you think coaching is appropriate.

1. Joe is a cashier and you are his shift supervisor at Tom's Tacos. The last few days you have noticed that Joe has been curt in his responses to some customers. Today, he even got into an argument with one customer over the price of the daily special. Joe has been with the business for two years and has a good work record. In the past he has been open to some

suggestions you have made, as long as they didn't require him to work more hours. You have time to meet with Joe after today's shift and you know he has the time as well. Based on the other factors, what would you do?

2. Last week you announced that the annual parts inventory would start next month and would require some extra work on the part of some employees. Samantha, who has been a parts clerk in the warehouse for six months, came to you and offered to do the extra work. She also expressed interest in learning more about the inventory process and taking responsibility for seeing that the inventory gets done right and on time. You have been looking for someone to take on some additional tasks to help you get ready for the inventory and to help. You hadn't thought of Samantha for the job. What would you do?

3. Ken, one of your service technicians, has been out on a service call for three hours. Based on the customer's description of the situation, it should have taken him thirty minutes to fix the problem and another thirty minutes of drive time to and from the job. You need to send him on another job. This is not the first time this has happened. Ken often seems to take longer than necessary on his service calls, especially considering his experience—he has ten years with the company. Many of the other service technicians look up to Ken and he is always telling them "war" stories about his experiences. What should you do?

Suggested Answers

1. You should schedule a coaching session with Joe today since time is available and before the situation gets worse. The performance problem is significant because it is affecting customer satisfaction, which can lead to lost sales and bad word-of-mouth advertising. Since he has been open to your suggestions in the past he is likely to be coachable.
2. You should meet with Samantha and find out exactly what she's interested in doing. This could be an opportunity to develop her skills. She may be able to take on more responsibilities that will make her a more valuable employee and also help you achieve your objectives. As her supervisor you can also be her coach and teach her new skills to make her feel better about her job and her accomplishments.
3. You may have let Ken's long service calls get out of hand. You need to schedule a coaching session with him as soon as possible. His behavior is affecting productivity. His influence with the other service technicians could lead to them doing the same thing on their calls. Given Ken's experience, it is important that you adopt the appropriate style when you talk to him. You also need to schedule enough time to adequately discuss the situation and take advantage of his experience.

The Coaching Process

The key to your coaching role as a first-line supervisor is to spend as much time as possible with your people each day. Avoid getting "chained" to your desk where you can't see first-hand how things are operating. Make a conscious effort at MBWA—management by walking around. The more contact you have with your employees, the better your chances of developing a relationship with them that encourages them to be open to your coaching efforts.

Training helps people gain the knowledge and skills needed to perform their jobs. When performance does not meet expectations, or when developmental goals and opportunities are missed, you have to switch to being a coach. Effective coaches know it is their responsibility to help their people get back on track. Good coaches also help people achieve their full potential.

A performance problem exists when there is a difference between the desired behavior and the actual behavior on the part of the employee. You may recognize a performance problem when one or more of the following conditions exist:

- Performance, which has been good, begins to slip.
- A person is having trouble keeping commitments or meeting deadlines.
- The person obviously needs help in resolving a problem.
- The person needs assistance in boosting performance to the next level.
- The person comes to you and asks for assistance.

Effective coaches use a four-step process to resolve these performance problems. Exhibit 4–3 shows this coaching process in more detail.

1. Get agreement that a problem exists.
2. Decide on a solution.
3. Follow up.
4. Give recognition when the problem is solved.

Exhibit 4–3
The Coaching Process

Get Agreement That a Problem Exists
- Ask questions to see whether the person is aware of the problem.
- Ensure that the person understands the consequences of the problem.
- Get agreement from the person that a problem exists.

Decide on a Solution
- Ask questions to involve the person with the problem.
- Generate as many alternatives to the problem as possible.
- Help the person think through the problem.
- Agree on the solution(s) that will be implemented.
- Agree on a timetable for implementation.

Follow Up
- Check to see whether the solution is implemented.
- Determine whether the solution is implemented on schedule.
- Determine whether the solution is working.

Give Recognition When the Problem is Solved
- Give specific feedback.
- Be sincere when you give feedback.
- Remember that recognition strengthens performance.

Keep in mind that this coaching process can also be used when an employee is doing an acceptable job but you both think performance could be even better. In this case, the first step is to get agreement on how the performance could be improved. Be as specific as possible in defining the expected results. Then steps 2 to 4 in the process are handled in the same manner as for an existing problem.

Each time you use this coaching process, for whatever reason, your goal should be to help your employees reach their full potential. When they reach their potential, you will be a more successful first-line supervisor.

Use the Coaching Worksheet in Exhibit 4–4 to develop a plan for coaching an employee with a specific performance problem. Think about any performance problems you currently are dealing with. After considering the significance factor, the time factor, and the coachability factor, select one performance problem that you want to resolve. Take a moment now to complete the top portion of the Coaching Worksheet.

Get Agreement That a Problem Exists

Agreeing that a problem exists can sometimes be the hardest step in the process. Few of us want to admit that we have a problem. We can easily see the problems other people are having, but it's more difficult to see our own. But until you can get the employee to agree that there is a problem, there's no point in going further in the process. You can't help people solve a problem if they don't think there is one.

Begin by asking questions to see whether the person is aware of the problem. You may have to ask several questions before you get any sort of agreement. Your questions should help the person understand the consequences of not solving the problem. For example, if you are dealing with an employee who is often late to work, some questions you might ask are:

- How many times have you been late in the last month?
- When was the last time you were late?
- How do you think other employees feel when you are late?
- How do you think I react when you are late?
- What happens to everyone's workload when you are late?
- How does being late affect your performance?

Listen to how the employee responds to each question. At some point in the discussion the person should begin to understand the effect being late has on those around him and agree that being late is a problem. Once you get agreement on the problem, you're ready to move on to the next step.

Take a moment to complete the "Getting Agreement" section of the Coaching Worksheet in Exhibit 4–4.

Decide on a Solution

Remember, your role as a coach is to *help* people solve their problems—not solve the problems for them. Therefore, in the second step of the process your goal is to get the employee to come up with an acceptable solution. As

Exhibit 4–4
Coaching Worksheet

Employee's Name _____ Date _____

Desired Performance: _____

_____

Actual Performance: _____

_____

Is the problem significant? Yes ____ No ____

Do you have time to coach? Yes ____ No ____

Is the employee coachable? Yes ____ No ____

1. **Get Agreement That a Problem Exists**
   - What questions might you ask the employee?

   _____

   _____

   _____

   _____

   - What consequences do you need to communicate to the employee?

   _____

   _____

   Key Point: Don't continue until you get agreement that a problem exists.

2. **Decide on a Solution**
   - What questions might you ask the employee?

   _____

   _____

   _____

   _____

   - What are some possible solutions you have thought of?

   _____

   _____

Exhibit continued on next page

© American Management Association. All rights reserved.
http://www.amanet.org/

Exhibit 4–4   continued from previous page

• What's an acceptable timetable for solving the problem?

3. Follow Up
   • When will you follow up to see whether the solution is implemented?

   • How will you determine whether the implementation is on schedule?

   • How will you determine whether the solution is working?

4. Give Recognition When the Problem Is Solved
   • What specific feedback can you give the employee?

   • What other types of recognition might be appropriate?

before, begin by asking questions. For example, you might ask, "What are some things you could do to ensure you are on time?"

Your questions should make the employee think of several different things that could be done to improve performance. Once several solutions have been identified, select the one(s) that will be implemented. In some situations, there may only be one solution; sometimes there will be several. Then set deadlines for implementing the solutions.

Now complete the "Decide on a Solution" section of the Coaching Worksheet in Exhibit 4–4.

Follow Up
All the time you spend getting agreement to a problem and deciding on a solution is wasted if you don't follow up. If you don't check to see whether the solution is implemented, you send a signal to the employee that the problem wasn't all that serious. Go out of your way to verify whether the employee tries out the agreed solution(s). Then, determine whether the solution is solving the problem.

If things go as planned, the problem should be eliminated or at least significantly reduced. If things haven't changed, you may want to schedule another meeting with the employee to verify implementation of the proposed solutions.

Now complete the "Follow Up" section of the Coaching Worksheet in Exhibit 4–4.

Give Recognition When the Problem Is Solved
Now is your opportunity to reinforce the employee's improved performance. Go out of your way to catch the employee doing something right. Be sincere and let the person know you appreciate the improved performance.

There's a saying that sums up this step: "Recognition strengthens performance." When you tell people you like the way they do things, you increase the chances that they'll continue to perform in the same way. If an employee who has been late starts coming to work on time, you need to recognize that change. Your recognition communicates to the employee that being on time really is important, and the employee is much more likely to continue to get to work on time.

Take a moment to complete the "Giving Recognition" section of the Coaching Worksheet in Exhibit 4–4.

When to Quit Coaching

As you have learned, coaching is hard work and can require a great deal of time and energy. Sometimes the return on the investment can be hard to determine. So, how long should you keep using your coaching skills to solve a performance problem? Or, put another way, when should you quit coaching? Since every situation is different, there is no one quick and simple answer. Every coaching situation has to be evaluated on its own merit. Jeffrey H. Davis (1995) suggests answering these questions before ending a coaching relationship:

- Has the employee's performance improved at all? If so, in what area?
- What is the employee's attitude toward work and the coaching relationship?
- Have you communicated expectations clearly?
- Have adequate training and follow-up support been provided for the employee?
- Was the performance improvement plan a realistic one?
- Have you consistently offered appreciation when the employee has performed well, and encouragement when the employee has failed or is facing difficult tasks?

recap

In this chapter you have looked at several of your first-line supervisory responsibilities for developing your people and helping them reach their full potential. You learned how to use new employee orientation as a development tool. You were given several suggestions on how to develop an orientation plan that takes advantage of a new employee's enthusiasm. The most important steps in implementing the orientation also were discussed.

Your role as a trainer was covered along with the four-step training method. This method can be applied to virtually any skill you need to teach your employees. Also presented were the characteristics of an effective trainer.

You also learned what you can do as a supervisor to make training stick with an employee. First, have a pre-training meeting followed by a post-training meeting. After the training you need to ensure the employee has the opportunity to perform, make sure there is a supportive environment for using the training, and then encourage and recognize improvements made as a result of the training.

We concluded the chapter with a discussion of how to be an effective coach. First, the factors to consider when deciding whether to coach employees were covered. Then you learned a four-step process you can use to help employees solve their problems.

As you put these new skills into practice, you will find that your people perform better and come closer to reaching their full potential. In the process, you'll find that you are more effective as a first-line supervisor.

Exercise 5: Taking It Back to the Workplace

INSTRUCTIONS: Now that you have completed the reading and the activities in this chapter, it's time to think specifically about how to apply what you have learned. The following questions are designed to help you consider what you need to do to succeed back in the workplace.

- ❑ What opportunities do you have for developing your employees?
- ❑ Have you developed a plan for new employee orientation?
- ❑ What method of training are you using with your employees?
- ❑ How well does your training "stick" with your employees?
- ❑ Are you taking advantage of all the coaching opportunities?
- ❑ What process are you using when coaching your employees?

Review Questions

1. What should be the goal of any employee development activity?
   (a) Save the company money
   (b) Help people reach their potential
   (c) Provide additional experience that can't be obtained on the job
   (d) Prepare employees for possible promotion or transfer

   1. (b)

2. An organized new employee orientation program saves supervisor time because it can:
   (a) all be delegated to someone else.
   (b) all be put in a book for the employee.
   (c) help reduce employee turnover.
   (d) be done by the human resources department.

   2. (c)

3. The correct sequence of the four-step training method is:
   (a) preparation, tryout, demonstration, follow-up.
   (b) presentation, demonstration, follow-up, tryout.
   (c) preparation, demonstration, follow-up, tryout.
   (d) preparation, presentation, tryout, follow-up.

   3. (d)

4. When demonstrating a task for the first time, you should do it:
   (a) slowly and in multiple phases.
   (b) at about 3/4 speed, as long as it looks fast to the employee.
   (c) at the speed you normally do it yourself.
   (d) at the speed you want the employee to do it.

   4. (d)

5. Which step is often the hardest in the coaching process?
   (a) Getting agreement that a problem exists
   (b) Deciding on a solution
   (c) Following up
   (d) Giving recognition when the problem is solved

   5. (a)

5

Managing People

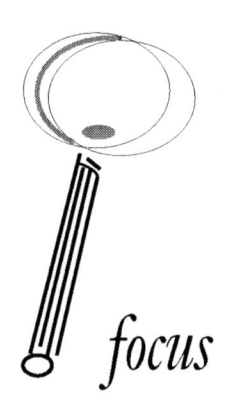

Learning Objectives

By the end of this chapter, you should be able to:

- Explain the importance of performance feedback and describe how to give both positive and corrective feedback.
- Identify and describe strategies for working with difficult employees.
- List causes of workplace conflict and explain how to manage conflict when it occurs.
- Describe the different methods for taking disciplinary action.

Managing employees can be a constant challenge for the first-line supervisor. Your primary concern has to be getting the job done and this has to be done through the efforts of your people. It is also likely that upper management is exhorting you to have your people work harder or more efficiently. There are performance standards to be met, and other departments are depending on the delivery of products or services.

In order to meet these multiple responsibilities, you have to focus on your responsibilities for managing people. This chapter provides guidance on the following people management skills:

1. Providing Performance Feedback
2. Working with Difficult Employees
3. Managing Workplace Conflict
4. Taking Disciplinary Action

Performance Feedback

Most people want and need regular feedback about their performance. In fact, it is estimated that 80 percent of the performance problems ("they just aren't motivated") that occur on the job would be solved if supervisors gave more and better feedback.

One of the reasons you see people rushing to leave work at the end of the day is that they are in a hurry to do something that gives them feedback. People spend their leisure time playing golf, bowling, fishing, or participating in activities where they get lots of feedback. How many people do you think would go to the bowling alley every week if they put a curtain in front of the pins? You would throw the first ball, hear a crash, and get your ball back. On your second shot you wouldn't know whether there was one pin or nine still behind the curtain. Bowling alleys that put up curtains would go out of business. Unfortunately for many people, work is that way—they never know whether they've knocked down one pin or gotten a strike.

It is estimated that people do things right 80 percent of the time, yet they rarely get positive feedback. Let them make a mistake, however, and someone is almost certain to let them know. Often when an employee is criticized and the feedback is not handled well, conflict results between the employee and the supervisor.

Using Feedback Systems

Feedback systems are methods of delivering performance data on a regular basis to employees about their work. Information may be in the form of production reports, error reports, sales numbers, budgets, or other measures you use to gauge the quality and/or quantity of work. Feedback systems are helpful for keeping employees informed about how they are doing and whether their performance is on target.

Feedback systems are not intended to replace personal, one-on-one feedback. However, they can be effective management tools by letting employees know where they stand in relation to specific goals. As a first-line supervisor you can use these systems as points of discussion. Clearly seeing the results provides common ground for you and your employees to view performance and for you to provide feedback on that performance.

Feedback systems can also be a source of "friendly competition" among employees. For example, if there are multiple shifts doing similar work they can compete with each other for the best results. Similarly, when there are multiple locations an organization often compares results from the various locations. Individual employees can also compare their performance with each other as well as from one week to the next.

Paul manages a service business that operates twenty-four hours a day. He has three eight-hour shifts, and each has a shift manager. Each quarter all three shifts set goals for themselves in terms of sales, customer satisfaction, quality, employee retention, and profit. He posts a big goal poster on the bulletin board in the employee break room. Each shift's goals are listed along with its current results. Each week he recognizes the shift that comes closest to its goals as well as the shift with the best results. His feedback system has created friendly competition and, even more importantly, more consistent results.

✎ Exercise 1: Feedback Systems

INSTRUCTIONS: Take a moment to think about the feedback systems you currently use or ones that you could develop.

Current System	What It Measures	How Often Used	Is It Effective?
_____	_____	_____	_____
_____	_____	_____	_____
_____	_____	_____	_____

New System	It Would Measure	How Often Used	Would It Be Effective?
_____	_____	_____	_____
_____	_____	_____	_____
_____	_____	_____	_____

Provide Positive Feedback to Reinforce Performance

It's human nature to want to please the boss. It's also human nature to want to be appreciated for doing a good job. Praise can take many different forms: a verbal thank-you, a written thank-you, recognition in front of peers, and rewards such as plaques or bonuses.

Giving feedback doesn't take much time and it isn't costly. When used appropriately, it can help keep your people on track and encourage them to continue good performance or improve poor performance. Effective praise has several elements—it's specific, immediate, earned, and individualized.

Be as Specific as Possible
Tell the employee what you liked and you are more likely to see that behavior again. "Janet, I really like the way you improved the efficiency of the production line by putting spare parts next to the line." Specific feedback of this type is a lot better than just saying, "Good job."

Feedback Should Be Immediate
The closer the feedback to the performance, the more impact it has. Don't wait for two or three days. Tell the employee as soon as possible.

Feedback Must Be Earned

Don't go around telling all your employees they did a good job just to give positive feedback. False praise can have a negative effect on the employee who knows he doesn't deserve it. It can also produce resentment among other employees who think you can't tell the difference between good and bad performance.

Individualize the Feedback

Use the person's name so he or she knows you recognized his or her specific contribution. Avoid saying the same thing to every employee. Be aware of individual differences; some employees may prefer verbal feedback whereas others would rather have it in writing. The more you know about your employees, the better you'll be at giving effective feedback that meets their needs.

It is important that you get in the habit of providing positive feedback on a regular basis. To help build the habit, you may want to:

- Put recognition on your daily "to do" list.
- Use voice mail and e-mail to send people recognition when you are away and can't do it in person.
- Use colorful note cards and write short positive comments on them and give them to the person. You'll be surprised how many will keep them as reminders.

✎ Exercise 2: Recognition and Reward

INSTRUCTIONS: Take a moment to complete this exercise now. You might also talk to some other first-line supervisors in your organization and ask them what they do to recognize and reward their employees.

Part I. Non-Monetary Recognition and Rewards

Your organization may provide monetary bonuses or other incentives to reward employee performance. However, as a first-line supervisor you also play a key role in motivating your employees by recognizing and rewarding their good performance. There are numerous *non-monetary* rewards you can give to create an environment where people feel respected and appreciated for a job well done. Add your own ideas to the following list:

- Greet employees as they arrive for work.
- Thank employees personally for doing extra work on a project.
- Recognize employees publicly at a team meeting.
- Send out a memo praising an employee's contribution.

- _____
- _____
- _____
- _____

- _____
- _____
- _____
- _____
- _____
- _____

Part II. Recognition Strengthens Performance

The use of frequent recognition is an important performance management tool. Letting people know you appreciate their work can lead to even better performance. List below those employees who deserve some positive feedback from you, the specific performance you want to recognize, and what you will say to the employee.

Employee: _____

Performance: _____

I will say: _____

Employee: _____

Performance: _____

I will say: _____

Employee: _____

Performance: _____

I will say: _____

Providing Corrective Feedback

Most people are aware when they have done something wrong but may not understand the effect of their behavior. That's why corrective feedback that solves the problem should be your goal. Corrective feedback should focus on unsatisfactory performance and how it can be eliminated. It should include four things: behavior, effect, expectation, and result.

Corrective feedback should focus on the unacceptable *behavior* (what the employee is doing or not doing). It is important that you keep the focus on the behavior, not on the person. Focusing on the person can lead to bias in the feedback, due to perceptions you may have for or against that person. Second, the corrective feedback should also explain the *effect*, that is, why the behavior is unacceptable, how it hurts productivity, or how it bothers others. Again, be sure you focus on the behavior and not the person. Then tell the employee what you *expect*. As noted earlier, when people know what you want, there is a better chance that they'll do it. Finally, let the employee know the *result*, that is, what will happen if behavior changes. Try to be positive whenever possible. In some cases, however, you may have to explain the negative consequences if the behavior continues. For example:

"John, it really causes a problem when you are late (behavior) because we get behind on production (effect). I expect you to be here on time every day (expectation). That way you can participate in our daily production decisions (result)." If the positive approach doesn't work, you may have to resort to negative consequences: "If you are late again I will have to dock your pay."

The goal when giving corrective feedback is to eliminate the behavior that caused the problem. When giving corrective feedback, avoid such terms as "never" or "always." These tend to make it sound like the person only does what's wrong and that you haven't seen any signs of the correct behavior. Also, give corrective feedback in private. Public criticism embarrasses the person and is usually rejected when someone else is around.

After giving corrective feedback, it's important that you follow up. Without follow-up you won't know whether the behavior has changed. When you do follow up, provide positive feedback if the performance has improved. If the performance is still unacceptable, however, repeat the corrective feedback.

Exercise 3: Giving Corrective Feedback

INSTRUCTIONS: The goal of giving corrective feedback is to eliminate the behavior that caused the problem. Take a moment to think about a specific situation in which you need to provide corrective feedback to an employee. Use the worksheet below to plan your corrective feedback.

Employee: _____

1. What is the *behavior* that needs to be corrected? Be specific.

_____

_____

2. What *effect* is the behavior having on others?

_____

_____

3. What do you *expect* the employee to do?

_____

_____

4. What will be the *result* if the behavior changes? If it doesn't change?

___

___

How and when will you follow up to see whether the behavior has improved?

___

___

Performance Appraisal as a Feedback Tool

How do you feel when your boss says it's time for your performance appraisal? Do you react with fear? Concern? Excitement? Enthusiasm? Whether it's your own performance that's being appraised or you are the one responsible for appraising an employee, performance appraisals never fail to bring out strong feelings.

One reason both supervisors and employees may feel this way is that they don't understand the purposes and benefits of the appraisal process. Effective performance appraisals have three purposes and benefits (Cadwell, 1994):

1. *Examine employee performance with respect to goals.* Performance appraisals tell both the supervisor and the employee how much progress they are making toward meeting established goals. It also gives you, as the supervisor, an opportunity to reinforce the expectations you have for the employee.
2. *Improve employee performance.* If an employee is having problems meeting his or her goals, you can take steps during the appraisal to help improve performance. Perhaps you need to provide additional resources or information. By working together, you and your employee should be able to ensure mutual goals are indeed met.
3. *Identify current or potential problems.* Sometimes employees have problems that they are not even aware of. Or perhaps something they are doing now is likely to result in a problem down the road. In either case, your role is to help your employees identify these current or potential problems. The performance appraisal process allows you to share your expertise about the ways things work in your organization.

Exhibit 5–1 provides an outline for the performance appraisal discussion process. Before you conduct a performance appraisal with an employee, you should talk to your immediate supervisor. It's important that you have a thorough understanding of the appraisal process in your organization and what is expected of you.

Numerous books, training workshops, and videos deal with the appraisal process in much more detail. The purpose of this chapter is to make you aware of the purposes and benefits of using performance appraisal as a performance management tool—not to provide you with comprehensive training in the appraisal process.

Exhibit 5-1
Performance Appraisal Discussion Process

Step 1: Control the Environment
- Schedule the meeting when and where you won't be interrupted
- Put the employee at ease

Step 2: State the Purpose of the Discussion
- Explain the purposes and benefits of the discussion
- Explain what information is being used for the discussion

Step 3: Ask for the Employee's Opinion
- Ask the employee to rate his own performance first
- Encourage participation by letting the employee know you are interested in his or her perspective
- Practice "active listening"

Step 4: Present Your Assessment
- Explain your assessment
- Explain your rationale for your assessment
- Provide positive feedback
- Provide corrective feedback

Step 5: Build on the Employee's Strengths
- Ask the employee to name his or her strengths
- Share your opinion of the employee's strengths
- Recap the strengths and relate them to performance goals

Step 6: Ask for the Employee's Reaction to Your Assessment
- Listen openly to the employee's responses
- Reach agreement on the rating

Step 7: Set Specific Goals
- Identify areas for improving performance
- Identify current training and development needs

Step 8: Close the Discussion
- Summarize the discussion
- Have the employee sign the appraisal form
- Thank the employee
- Explain what will happen next

WORKING WITH DIFFICULT EMPLOYEES

The term "difficult employees" is really a misnomer and doesn't do either employees or supervisors much good. What we really mean is that there are employees who have difficult *behaviors* from time to time that cause supervisors and even other employees to have a negative reaction. If we are honest with ourselves, we will probably admit that someone else could even sometimes describe us as being difficult. If you don't think so, ask your spouse, significant other, a friend, a parent, a son or daughter, or—if you really want to get risky—your boss. Most likely they can cite one or more incidents in which you were difficult. Therefore, this section focuses on behaviors that might be considered difficult—rather than some group of employees with an incorrect label.

Types of Difficult Behaviors

Difficult behaviors do not occur naturally in people (admittedly there may be a small fraction born with some mental disorder, but these are relatively few); instead, these difficult behaviors tend to be made. Some of the difficult behaviors you may observe in your employees from time to time are:

- Negative actions or words
- Non-productivity
- Sarcasm
- Unhappiness
- Untrustworthiness
- Poor attendance
- Poor listening
- Disruptiveness
- Unwillingness to make changes
- Lack of focus

Since these behaviors are outside of what we expect from our employees, we are quick to label the employees as difficult. Rather than hang that label on someone who may just be having a bad hour or a bad day, think about it in terms of the employee's specific behavior.

Causes of Difficult Behaviors

Why do some people exhibit these negative behaviors? In most cases they are the result of the environment they live and work in (yes, you could be the cause of the difficult behavior) as well as the pressures and stresses brought on by everyday living. One aspect that is different is that some people tend to exhibit these negative behaviors longer and more frequently than others. One reason is that the negative behaviors are not dealt with when they first appear. As a result they tend to feed on themselves and get worse as time goes on.

As a first-line supervisor you have to deal with the negative behaviors as soon as you become aware of them. You can't let them stretch out over several hours or even days. The longer they last, the more difficult they are to address. Dealing with negative behaviors in a timely and appropriate manner can improve morale and reduce internal conflicts. Unresolved, however, these behaviors seem to promote additional, similar problems, and people then become inclined toward less desirable behavior. Your action or inaction impacts whether the cycle remains negative or becomes positive. When negative behaviors are resolved in a positive way, the result is often improved morale and a better working environment.

As a first-line supervisor, you have the authority and power to deal with these difficult behaviors. Though you must act decisively, you should obtain all the facts before acting. Even if you have empathy, good communication skills, and an impartial attitude, you will not be able to eliminate all difficult behaviors. However, such attributes can and do make a difference when trying to deal with such behaviors.

Strategies for Working with Difficult Behaviors

You can use a number of procedures to address difficult behaviors without disrupting morale or performance. In certain situations, these procedures benefit morale. But keep in mind that any anger or other negative conduct on your part only escalates difficult behavior, reduces your ability to motivate, and cripples performance.

Focus on the Behavior

Remember what was said earlier—we aren't dealing with difficult employees, but with difficult behaviors. If you focus on the person, chances are he or she will react negatively. In some cases, the employee may even try to turn the tables on you and put the focus on you instead. It is important that you control your own emotions, remain calm, and focus on the behavior that needs to be addressed.

Use "I" Messages

One of the best techniques, and sometimes most difficult, is to replace the pronoun "you" with the pronoun "I." Instead of saying, "You really made me mad when you argued with that customer," try saying, "I really get mad when someone argues with me when I'm a customer." By the keeping the "you" out of the statement it puts the emphasis on the behavior not on the person. Putting it in terms of how it affects you ("I" in the example) also helps keep the discussion from becoming personal.

Determine the Cause of the Behavior

The best way to deal with the behavior is head-on. Don't beat around the bush. Begin by asking questions about the behavior. At this point still try to avoid using "you" and try to focus on what "I" or "we" can do about the behavior. Begin to demonstrate a commitment to help the person eliminate the behavior. Some questions you might use are:

- What caused the problem?
- What else could have been done?
- How would someone else have handled that?
- What can I do to help?
- When did the problem first occur?

Develop a Plan for Improvement

Once you have determined the cause of the difficult behavior, there needs to be a plan for improving or eliminating the behavior. The best plan is one that is made by the employee as long as it meets with your approval. The use of "you" is appropriate at this stage as you ask questions about what can be done. Now you want the employee to start thinking about what changes he or she will make. For example:

- What do you think we should do?
- What do you think would work best?
- What would you like to do?
- When do you plan to make the change?

Get a Commitment
Once the plan is decided on, get a commitment from the employee that the change will be made and when. If possible, of course, you want the change to be made immediately and the difficult behavior eliminated. There may be extenuating circumstances, however, that affect when the change can be implemented. In some cases (if the behavior has been happening for a long time) you may even want to get a written commitment. Generally, though, a verbal agreement is best because it doesn't seem as drastic to the employee. The key to making the commitment work is to follow up. Make sure you take time to verify that the difficult behavior has been eliminated.

Exercise 4: What Would You Do?

INSTRUCTIONS: Read each of the situations below and then briefly describe what you would do.

1. You received an e-mail this morning from Jill, who has worked in your department for three months. She complained that she had to work late the last two days to get her work done and that she wasn't going to do it again tonight. She complained about the workload and said that it was unfair for her to have to put in the extra hours. Furthermore, she said she was planning to leave an hour early today to make up for the extra hours she had worked. You know that she is exaggerating because she only worked an extra fifteen minutes on Monday and an extra thirty minutes on Tuesday. What would you do?

2. During your daily production meeting with Rod, he said he was having a problem getting employees to put their tools away at the end of their shifts. They say that since there is only one shift a day, putting their tools away and then getting them out again the next day wastes time. If they have to keep doing it, they say they will "slow down" their work for a couple of days. Rod said he agreed with the other employees and wants you to change the policy. Already, one expensive tool has turned up missing. What would you do?

Suggested Answers:

1. First, you need to set up a meeting with Jill to address the issue face to face. Don't respond to her e-mail and get into a back and forth exchange of e-mails that could go on all day. When you meet, ask her why she has been working the extra time and ask her for suggestions on how she could get her work done within normal hours. Then, ask what you can do to help. Together agree on a solution. You also need to get agreement on whether she will be leaving early today since she should have asked—not told—you about leaving early. Be sure to follow up on her commitment.

2. Tools are expensive and necessary in order to get the work done. The company can't afford to have them turn up missing. Call a shift meeting to clearly communicate the reasons behind the policy and make sure everyone understands it. Use "I" messages as much as possible and focus on the importance of following the policy. You may also want to ask the employees for their input on what you can do to help them ensure the policy is followed. Ask for their renewed commitment to the policy and then follow up to see that tools are put away at the end of today's shift.

MANAGING WORKPLACE CONFLICT

Conflict in the workplace may be inevitable. No matter how hard you try to keep everyone focused, provide regular feedback, and deal with issues in a timely manner, conflict occurs. Unresolved conflicts can contribute to poor performance. As a first-line supervisor, you have the responsibility and obligation to settle many conflicts. Failure to do so may only worsen the conflict.

Keep in mind, however, that some conflict can be healthy. Although our initial reaction is usually that conflict is a negative thing, it can be a good sign. When there is no conflict it can be sign that people are complacent, bad ideas are not challenged, and people aren't being totally honest with each other. In this section we take a look at some of the common causes of conflict and some of the things you can do when it happens.

Causes of Conflict

Understanding why conflict occurs is necessary in order to be able to manage conflict situations in an effective manner. What follows is not intended to be an exhaustive list, but rather some of the more common causes of workplace conflict.

Different Priorities

Sometime employees have different ideas about what is the most important priority. For example, two employees may be working on different parts of the same project. Each may think that their part is the highest priority. A conflict can arise over who should have access to resources first in order to get the assigned part of the project done.

Making Assumptions

Conflicts often arise when one person makes an assumption about another person's actions or intentions. Rather than communicating with the other person, the first person assumes he or she knows what the other person is thinking or planning to do. When he or she acts on assumptions that turn out to be wrong, a conflict can occur. Sometimes this conflict can be imaginary because the first person has created a conflict in his or her mind based on an incorrect assumption.

Different Values

A conflict can occur when two people put a different value on something. For example, one person may value getting things done as quickly as possible regardless of the quality. When that person is assigned to work with someone who thinks that quality is more important than speed, their different values can lead to conflict. Or, one person thinks the way a person dresses at work is important whereas another person thinks getting the job done is more important than how one is dressed.

Different Knowledge/Experience

Different levels of knowledge and experience can also cause conflict. One person may make a decision based on previous knowledge and experience. The decision seems obvious and logical to that person. Someone with a different level of knowledge or experience, however, may not understand why the decision was made. Based on their own knowledge and experience, they would make a different decision. Unless they are willing to discuss their reasons with each other, the conflict likely won't be resolved.

Different Personalities

People are different—that's a statement of the obvious. It would be boring if we were all the same. Many of the differences among people are positive and make for good working relationships because people skills, abilities, and interests complement each other. It's also a fact that different personalities can lead to conflicts. One person takes everything very seriously whereas another seems to find humor in every situation. Put these two people together and conflict may result.

Different Perceptions

People see things differently, which can lead to conflict. One person sees problems as something to be avoided at all costs. Another person welcomes problems because he or she enjoys the challenge of solving them. As the saying goes, one person sees the glass half empty while the other sees it as half full. Their differing perceptions can lead to doing different things.

Conflict Management Styles

Your approach to resolving your own conflicts is likely to be the same approach you use when trying to resolve a conflict between two of your employees. Being aware of your preferred conflict management style can be helpful as you try to resolve conflicts. Listed below are five conflict management styles that you might use to resolve a conflict you have with another person. One style is not necessarily better than another. You may find that you need to consider using a different conflict management style than the one you prefer, based on the nature of the conflict. In other words, you may have to adapt your style to resolve the conflict.

Competition
A person pursues his or her own concerns in a confrontational, assertive, and aggressive manner. This is a power-oriented role, in which a person uses whatever power seems appropriate to win—based on his or her ability to argue, having a higher rank, or using economic sanctions. Competing might mean survival of the fittest, defending a position you believe is correct, or simply trying to win to prove one's own superiority.

Accommodation
This is the opposite of competition. This person is agreeable and non-assertive because he or she does not want to risk damaging relationships. When accommodating, an individual is cooperative even at the expense of personal goals. There is an element of self-sacrifice. Accommodating might include obeying another person's order when one would prefer not to, or yielding to another's point of view.

Avoidance
The person is non-confrontational and ignores or passes over issues. He or she denies there is a problem and tends to view differences as too minor or too great to resolve. He or she thinks that attempting to solve the conflict could create even greater problems. Avoiding might take the form of diplomatically sidestepping an issue, postponing an issue until a better time, or simply withdrawing from a threatening situation.

Collaboration
This is the opposite of avoiding. There is high respect and mutual support between parties. Collaborating involves an attempt to work with the other person to find some solution that fully satisfies the concerns of both. It means openly discussing an issue to identify the underlying concerns of the two individuals and finding a mutually beneficial solution. Collaborating can be both assertive and cooperative as two people openly explore a disagreement in order to find a creative solution. The goal is to resolve the conflict that would otherwise have them competing for resources.

Compromise
The objective is to find some expedient, mutually acceptable solution that partially satisfies both parties. It falls in a middle ground between competing and accommodating. This person says that no one person or idea is perfect and that there is more than one good way to do anything. Compromise gives up more than competing but less than accommodating. Likewise, it

addresses an issue more directly than avoiding, but doesn't explore it in as much depth as collaborating. Compromising can include splitting the differences, exchanging concessions, or seeking a middle-ground position.

These style descriptions are adapted from the Thomas-Kilmann Conflict Mode Instrument by Kenneth W. Thomas and Ralph H. Kilmann. The instrument and related support materials are available from various sources on the Internet.

✎ Exercise 5: What's Your Conflict Management Style?

INSTRUCTIONS: Think about your own preferred conflict management style, and answer the following questions.

What is your preferred conflict management style?

___

What are the advantages of your preferred style?

___

What are the disadvantages of your preferred style?

___

What other style(s) would be useful? Why?

___

Steps for Successful Conflict Management

Regardless of the style you choose, your long-term objective is to resolve the conflict so that it does not become destructive to you, your employees, or the workplace. Let's look at a process you can use when resolving conflicts.

Step 1: Take the Initiative to Resolve the Conflict

Some conflicts may go away if you avoid them, but most won't. Instead it's up to you to take responsibility for resolving the conflict. Your willingness to get involved communicates that you think it is important to have a workplace environment where people can get along and work together.

If those who are in conflict don't come to you, go to them and let them know you are aware of the conflict. Explain that you want to *help them* resolve the situation. This is an important point. As the supervisor it is not your job to resolve the conflict. Your role is to be the mediator. You may, depending on the situation, offer some suggestions, but the main responsibility for solving the conflict has to be on the shoulders of those who are in conflict.

Step 2: Determine the Cause of the Conflict

Once you get those in conflict together, you have to determine the cause of their conflict. This may not be easy. It takes time and energy to get agreement on the cause of the conflict. You likely will have to deal with the emotions of the people involved. Let people express their feelings. This is a good time to get everything out on the table. There may even be multiple causes for the conflict. There are four steps you can take to help determine the cause of the conflict:

1. Establish ground rules
2. Ask questions
3. Listen
4. Maintain focus on solving the problem

1. *Establish ground rules.* Before people start talking you have to establish the ground rules to be followed during the discussion. Here are some ground rules you should consider for everyone involved:
   - Be open and honest.
   - Listen to the other person.
   - Avoid being argumentative.
   - State the facts and avoid opinions and feelings.
   - Respect each other's position.

2. *Ask questions.* Open-ended questions and probing questions and/or statements are needed to determine the real cause of the problem. Don't be hesitant to follow up on what someone says with another question. Some examples are:
   - What do you think caused the conflict?
   - Why do you say that?
   - Tell me more about that.
   - What happened when you did that?
   - How do you think (other person) feels about that?
   - What do you think we should do now?
   - How do you think others will feel if we do that?

3. *Listen.* Your listening skills are critical. It's important that you hear what is being said and the meaning behind what is being said. Review the effective listening techniques in Chapter 3. Your ability to listen and maintain an open mind is essential if you want to get to the real cause of the conflict.

4. *Maintain focus on solving the problem.* When emotions, feelings, and opinions are involved it is easy to get sidetracked. Your job is to help maintain the proper focus. Here are some things you can do:
   - Focus on ideas, not personalities.
   - Acknowledge the merits of various points of view.
   - Give people time to think as well as to talk.
   - Respect people's opinions.
   - Keep focused on the problem at hand.

Step 3: Develop an Action Plan

Next, develop an action plan based on addressing what has been determined to be the cause of the conflict. Involve both parties in developing an action plan. As the supervisor, your role is to make sure the plan is acceptable to both parties and to yourself. Avoid letting one person dominate the development of the plan, otherwise the conflict is likely to recur or take on another form. If you have done a good job determining the cause of the conflict, the action required to resolve the conflict should be pretty obvious. The plan does not need to be elaborate, but it should answer the following questions:

- What changes will be made?
- Who will do what?
- If the conflict cannot be resolved immediately, what is the timeline?

Step 4: Follow Up

Don't assume that just because there was agreement to a plan to resolve the conflict that everything will get back on track immediately. Conflicts that have built up over time are likely to require some time to be resolved. Make sure you take time to check back with both parties and find out how things are going. Start with individual meetings. If you still sense some underlying conflict, you may want to get them back together and repeat step three.

Once you are confident that the conflict has been resolved, as part of your follow-up provide positive feedback. This reinforces the changed behaviors and lets both parties know that you have noticed what they have done.

✎ Exercise 6: Resolving Workplace Conflict

INSTRUCTIONS: Describe a workplace conflict that you had to help resolve.

_____

_____

What was the cause of the conflict?

_____

_____

What process did you use to resolve the conflict?

_____

_____

Has the conflict recurred? Why or why not?

_____

_____

What new ideas do you have after reading this chapter?

_____

_____

TAKING DISCIPLINARY ACTION

The whole concept of discipline has a negative connotation. We can give it a fancy name like performance improvement, constructive discipline, or positive discipline, but in the end it still doesn't sound like much fun. So let's face the reality—taking disciplinary action isn't much fun. But then, it shouldn't be. When a supervisor has to take disciplinary action it may not just be because of what the *employee* did or didn't do, it may also be a result of something the *supervisor* did or didn't do. In the final analysis, good employee performance is often the result of good supervision.

Focus on Behavior

There will be times that no matter how well you do your job as a supervisor, some employees won't do what they are supposed to do and you have to take disciplinary action. There are two reasons for taking disciplinary action: to eliminate current undesirable behavior, and to prevent undesirable behavior in the future.

Throughout this chapter the focus has been on behavior—what the employee is doing that needs to be changed or eliminated. When taking disciplinary action, this is especially important. Avoid discussions that talk about the attitudes and the feelings of an employee; instead, stick to the behaviors you can observe. Otherwise the disciplinary discussion can become contentious and counterproductive.

Whenever you have a meeting with an employee to discuss behavior issues, document the meeting and place the documentation in the employee's file. Some organizations have specific forms that are used for this purpose. If your organization does not, be sure the documentation you create has the date, a summary of what was discussed and agreed to, and both your and the employee's signatures. This documentation can protect both you and your organization from unjustified claims for unemployment compensation and from complaints of discrimination or unfair labor practices. Exhibit 5–2 describes the steps to follow when taking disciplinary action.

Disciplinary Options

You can use several options when taking disciplinary action. Let's look at them briefly:

- Oral Warning
- Written Warning
- Suspension
- Termination

Exhibit 5-2
Taking Disciplinary Action

Here are some steps you should follow to conduct a professional disciplinary action meeting with an employee:

1. Meet with the employee
   A. Restate the problem behavior
   B. Refer to past conversations or agreements
   C. State why the behavior is still a problem
   D. Inform the employee of his status
   E. Set deadlines for improvement

2. Document the meeting
   A. Fill out required paperwork
   B. Have the employee sign the documentation
   C. Place documentation in the employee's file

3. Follow up
   A. Check back to see whether behavior has changed
   B. Provide recognition for improvement

Some organizations refer to these as steps in a progressive disciplinary process because the severity of the discipline increases with each option. First the employee gets an oral warning. If that doesn't fix the behavior, a written warning follows. If the problem persists, then the employee is suspended. If the behavior still isn't corrected, the employee is terminated. In some organizations, the nature of the behavior or the circumstances surrounding the behavior may sometimes dictate that action not follow this sequence. In some cases, suspension or even termination may be the first disciplinary action.

Oral Warning

An oral warning is used to let employees know that their behavior is unacceptable. Before you give an oral warning, you should use the corrective feedback process described earlier in this chapter. If the employee's behavior does not improve following the corrective feedback, the oral warning serves as a stronger action. In this case you are warning the employee that his or her behavior must change. You should also make it clear that if the behavior doesn't change, further disciplinary action will be taken. Remember the goal of giving the oral warning is to eliminate the unacceptable behavior.

Written Warning

In most cases you use a written warning after an oral warning has been given and there has been no change in behavior. The written warning lets the employee know that you still consider the behavior to be a serious problem. As its name implies, be sure to document the warning in writing. The documentation should follow a private meeting with the employee in which you focus on the behavior. If you have previous documentation about the behavior in question, review it at the meeting. When you give a written warning, be sure the employee understands what can happen next if the behavior does not change. Sometimes an employee's behavior may improve after a written warning for an extended period of time. However, if the problem returns in the future you may want to repeat the written warning.

Suspension

Suspension is used when an employee has flagrantly violated an organization's policy, or when you have reason to believe that a policy has been violated and you need time to investigate. In either case the employee should be asked to leave the premises. Suspension allows you to cool down if you are upset and it also allows time to conduct any necessary investigation into the behavior. The employee may or may not be paid during the suspension, depending on the organization's policy. Depending on the results of the investigation, the employee may be reinstated, reassigned, or terminated. Suspension allows you to handle employee behavior problems in a timely and mature manner while at the same time ensuring that employees receive fair treatment.

Termination

Involuntary termination is a task most supervisors would rather avoid. The best way to avoid it is to focus on behavior problems when they first occur and before they get to an inappropriate level. Involuntary terminations may be necessary due to business conditions or for cause. Business conditions may include the elimination of a job or a temporary layoff. An employee may be terminated for cause when he has not responded to previous efforts to improve behavior or following a suspension when you find there is reason to terminate the employee. Before terminating an employee, be sure you have:

- Gathered the facts and previous documentation
- Discussed the situation with your supervisor
- Set a time and place for the termination meeting
- Completed all necessary paperwork

In most cases, involuntary termination is only used after repeated attempts to get the employee to change behavior using one or more of the other disciplinary actions.

You may also have to deal with voluntary terminations—when the employee makes the decision to quit. Most organizations have policies and procedures they follow for voluntary terminations, depending on the circumstances of the termination and the employee's future plans. Some common alternatives are to have the employee quit working immediately, leave on a date desired by the employee, or leave on a date agreed to by both the organization and the employee. As with involuntary terminations, be sure you complete all necessary paperwork and follow your organization's procedures. Sometimes you may leave the "door open" for the employee to return in the future, so be sure you handle the termination process in a professional manner.

✎ Exercise 7: Taking Disciplinary Action

INSTRUCTIONS: Answer the following questions based on your own experience with disciplinary action.

What is your organization's policy for disciplinary action?

_____

_____

What types of disciplinary action have you had to take?

_____

_____

Could the disciplinary action have been avoided? If so, how?

_____

_____

What, if anything, did you do or not do that contributed to the need to take disciplinary action?

_____

_____

What did you learn from the experience?

_____

_____

recap

This chapter discussed the importance of managing people. First, we examined the role of feedback in managing people. The use of feedback systems was discussed along with techniques for giving positive feedback. We also discussed the importance of using non-monetary rewards to motivate employees. Good first-line supervisors also use corrective feedback to motivate performance by focusing on an employee's *behavior*, the *effect* of their behavior, the *expectation* for their performance, and the *result*—what will happen if behavior changes. The use of performance appraisal as a feedback tool was also discussed.

In the next part you learned that there are employees who exhibit difficult *behaviors* from time to time that cause supervisors and even other employees to have a negative reaction to them. You read about different types of difficult behaviors, the causes of difficult behaviors, and strategies for working with employees with difficult behaviors.

Next you learned about the possible causes of workplace conflicts. You learned about different ways to approach conflict and techniques you can use. You were also given a four-step process to follow to resolve workplace conflicts: take the initiative to resolve the conflict, determine the cause of the conflict, develop an action plan, and follow up.

Finally, we looked at taking disciplinary action. You learned about the importance of focusing on eliminating undesirable behavior. The options of oral warning, written warning, suspension, and termination were discussed. You were also reminded to follow your organization's policies when taking disciplinary action.

Exercise 8: Taking It Back to the Workplace

INSTRUCTIONS: Now that you have completed the reading and the activities in this chapter, it's time to think specifically about how to apply what you have learned. The following questions are designed to help you consider what you need to do to succeed back in the workplace.

- What opportunities do you have to provide more positive feedback to your employees?
- What type of feedback systems are you using?
- How do you deal with employees with difficult behaviors?
- How effective are you in resolving workplace conflicts?
- What conflict management style do you use most often? How could you benefit from using a different style?
- What process have you used when you have had to take disciplinary action?

Review Questions

1. Which of the following are elements of effective praise?
   (a) Specific, immediate, earned, and group-oriented
   (b) Immediate, earned, positive, and general
   (c) Specific, immediate, earned, and individualized
   (d) General, immediate, earned, and individualized

   1. (c)

2. Performance appraisal can be an effective feedback tool because it allows you to:
   (a) keep people from getting too far ahead of others.
   (b) compare employees to each other to control pay rates.
   (c) determine which employees can be promoted out of your department.
   (d) build on an employee's strengths and abilities.

   2. (d)

3. When dealing with difficult employees it is most important to focus on their:
   (a) attitude.
   (b) behavior.
   (c) tenure.
   (d) position.

   3. (b)

4. Which conflict management style would you use if you were most concerned about both yourself and the other person?
   (a) Collaboration
   (b) Compromise
   (c) Avoidance
   (d) Competition

   4. (a)

5. If an employee is flagrantly violating a company policy and you are upset about the situation, your best course of action would be to:
   (a) give the employee an oral warning.
   (b) give the employee a written warning.
   (c) suspend the employee and investigate.
   (d) terminate the employee immediately.

   5. (c)

6

Building a Team

focus

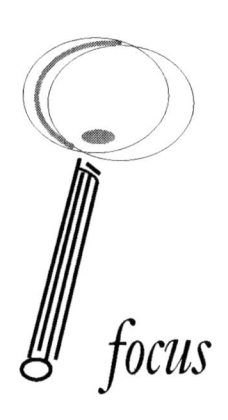

Learning Objectives

By the end of this chapter you should be able to:

- Describe the benefits of teamwork.
- Define what a team is.
- List the steps required to transform a group into a team.
- Identify the ten keys to being a valuable team member.
- List obstacles to team development and explain how to overcome them.

Since first appearing on this planet, humans have formed themselves together in groups. The basic groups were families, which were necessary for protection, sustenance, and rearing children. Families joined together to form bands or tribes. Through the ages, humans have formed groups for economic, political, educational, and religious reasons. Sometimes groups work together effectively and sometimes they do not. When group members recognize the importance of working together, a significant shift occurs: They are no longer just groups; they become teams.

When Kamile was promoted to a supervisor's position she took over a department of seven bookkeepers. During the interview process she had been told one of the reasons they wanted someone new to supervise the department was that although there were several good people, they never seemed to be "on the same page." She was told that they often seemed to be at odds with each other and with their current supervisor. When Kamile accepted the job offer, her boss told her that he expected her to make them a team. Kamile's challenge is one that most supervisors, new and experienced, have heard at one time or another. This chapter prepares you for the challenge of building a team.

Why Teamwork?

Almost every management text or article you read or management expert you hear states that teamwork is essential to success. The value of teamwork is evident in sporting events, in social and political groups, and in many business organizations. Yet teamwork often falls apart in many organizations due to impatience, personal jealousies, indifference, and internal competition.

As Kamile and others have found, teamwork doesn't happen automatically. It takes hard work, cooperation, training, and the willingness to accept personal risks, make changes, and put aside personal desires so the team's objectives can be achieved.

Organization Benefits

Each year in this country, thousands of groups form teams for athletic competition. Some of these groups never make the transition to a team and their performance reflects the contributions of individuals, not a team effort. Those who make the transition reap much more substantial benefits. Such benefits accrue not just to sports teams but also to teams in the workplace. The benefits of teamwork are as follows:

- Teams can accomplish more with less waste.
- Teams can produce better quality more efficiently.
- Team members have opportunity for personal development.
- Teams can often be more flexible in how they approach tasks.
- Teams members develop confidence and trust in each other.
- Teamwork takes advantage of the synergy of the efforts of all team members.
- Teams focus on performance; they are concerned about results and what they can accomplish.

Although these benefits may seem obvious to you, don't assume that everyone in your group perceives them or values them. Merely listing these benefits somewhere or telling everyone about them will not help you develop your team. You have to prove through daily experience that the group, working together as a team, will reap the benefits. As these benefits become apparent to your people, it becomes easier to maintain a team atmosphere. What other organization benefits can you think of?

_____

_____

_____

Individual Benefits

Being involved with a team invariably leads people to a better understanding of the overall purpose of the work group and the organization. Upper management usually perceives members of effective teams more positively.

Through team participation, they are better able to demonstrate their abilities and their commitment to productivity.

Teamwork helps people learn from each other and demonstrate additional skills that may be of value to the organization. Through delegation of tasks, individuals develop interpersonal skills and understanding and have the opportunity to take on challenging responsibilities. Team members also have greater flexibility to devise alternative ways of doing things. When a team is successful, all its members improve their self-images and confidence to meet future challenges.

One way to take advantage of these benefits is to have your people work together as often as possible. Have them focus on group goals while meeting individual responsibilities. When they see team goals being achieved, they are even more encouraged to achieve their individual goals.

If your group is involved with piecework or commission sales that emphasize individual performance, it may be more difficult to promote teamwork. Be sure employees understand how individual success can contribute to the team's success. In almost all cases, one of the major benefits of promoting a team spirit is the reduction of internal competition and conflict.

Providing recognition and appreciation for group and individual accomplishments inspires the pride necessary for team spirit. As the group works together, members learn from each other and understand each other better. Individual skills become group assets, rather than sources of disruptive competition. How have you personally benefited from being a team member?

_____

_____

_____

WHAT IS A TEAM?

A *team* has been defined as "a small number of people with complementary skills who are committed to a common purpose, performance goals, and approach for which they hold themselves mutually accountable" (Katzenbach and Smith, 1994). Let's look at each part of the definition and see what it takes to be an effective team. As we do, think about your own work teams and how they compare.

- *Small Number of People.* A team can be as few as two people or, as in the case of some football teams, close to 100. When teams get too large, they are often subdivided into smaller teams. In football, for example, there is the offense, the defense, the special teams, etc. In the workplace if you get too many people involved it can be hard to make progress. Although there is no ideal number, once you get more than ten to twelve people on a team, it can be hard to keep everyone focused, and you may need to subdivide your team.

How many people are on your team(s)? What adjustments, if any, do you need to make?

___
___
___

- *Complementary Skills.* Team members need to bring different strengths to the team. If everyone has the same strengths (or weaknesses) the team tends to get bogged down time and again in the same areas. You need a mix of people who are analytical, creative, impulsive, controlled, etc. Of course, as the team leader, it is your job to ensure that you have the right mix of skills so the team performs well and meets its objectives.

What skill sets do your team members have? What skills are missing? What skills are overabundant?

___
___
___

- *Purpose and Goals.* Do your team members know what is expected of them? Teams must have a reason for being and that reason must be clear to all members. If they don't know what their purpose is, they won't be able to move forward. It's been said, "If you don't know where you are going, any road will take you there." An effective team must have a clear sense of direction and know what is expected of it in reaching its goals.

What is the stated purpose of your team? How many team members can state the purpose as well as you can?

___
___
___

- *Common Approach.* Team members need to agree on how they will work together to achieve their goals. Often this is accomplished by establishing a set of ground rules and expectations that are clear for everyone. All team members need to be aware of their responsibilities, the roles they are expected to play, with whom they are to work, how much authority they have, and what other people's expectations are. Having this common knowledge is essential to getting everyone on the same page and working together.

Does your team have established ground rules? What is its level of authority? What is it expected to accomplish?

___
___
___

- *Mutual Accountability.* Effective teams are made up of members who hold each other accountable. Members expect to report their results to the team and to explain what they did and why. They realize that being open and honest with each other is critical to success. Individuals who want to "do their own thing" have a tough time working on teams. Team success comes from a willingness to be involved in the give and take among team members that calls on each person to account for their actions.

Do your team members hold each other accountable? Are people required to report regularly to the team and to explain their actions?

_____

_____

_____

Transforming a Group into a Team

Being aware of what constitutes a team is the first step in making the transition from a group to a team. The next step is to do those things that build an effective team.

This was the challenge that Kamile faced. In her first group meeting she quickly observed what others had been telling her. The people were enthusiastic and committed, but they didn't agree on the priorities or what they should be doing. Consequently, they did not work together. Each person was focused on his or her specific tasks without regard for what the others were doing. Kamile realized that to transform her group into a team was going to take some time and effort.

Team building is a complex process that, to be successful, requires time, commitment, and organization support. Before you embark on the team building process, be sure you are willing to do the work necessary and can obtain the necessary resources.

Effective supervisors know that teamwork means sharing three things with their people: expectations, responsibilities, and glory. Effective first-line supervisors make sure their people know what is expected, they know what their responsibilities are, and they get the glory when goals are achieved.

Share the Expectations

Employees have to know what you expect. Whether it's the job to be done today or the goals for the next six months, your role as a first-line supervisor is to tell employees what is expected. As you learned in Chapter 3, if you don't clearly communicate expectations, you may not get the specific results you want.

When you share your expectations, don't be afraid to ask employees for their input and listen to what they have to say. Give them an opportunity to provide feedback and make suggestions on ways to accomplish the expected results. This is a good way to keep them involved and to make them feel part of your team.

Use your active listening skills to let your employees know you are listening to their suggestions. Write down their comments and try to determine what changes, if any, they need to make as a team in order to meet the expectations. When everyone has the same understanding of what's expected, results are a lot easier to achieve.

After her initial meeting with her group, Kamile decided that what they really needed was a clear understanding of what their function was in the organization. Kamile met with her boss and got his insight. Then she went back to the team and shared her expectations for the department. She didn't stop there. She also asked her people for their ideas. Over the course of the meeting they reached agreement on what their primary roles should be. It took a couple of more meetings before everyone was on board, but eventually they developed a set of written expectations and objectives that everyone agreed with: They were beginning to think more like a team.

What expectations have you communicated to your team?

_____

_____

_____

Share the Responsibilities

You need to use several skills when sharing responsibilities. Perhaps the most important is delegation, which is covered in detail in Chapter 7. Effective first-line supervisors know that achieving organizational goals is not something they can do by themselves. They understand the importance of sharing responsibility for each component of the goal. This involves everyone in the process and normally results in more being done.

After the tasks have been assigned, the next step is to establish a system to help monitor and ensure results are achieved. The system should be simple yet carefully designed not to so restrict an employee's freedom of action that it undercuts motivation. In some cases it can be as simple as a written report or a meeting in which people report their results to the team.

Kamile's approach was to turn the department expectations into specific goals. It was clear that if all the goals were achieved, the department would meets its expectations. Then she let the team members decide for themselves who would be responsible for what goals. The result was that people took responsibility for what they did best. In some cases it was necessary for two or more people to work together to achieve a goal. When they were done everyone had assumed some degree of responsibility for helping the department meets its goals.

How have you shared your responsibilities with your team?

_____

_____

_____

Share the Glory

Leaders who forget to share the glory often find that their people quickly lose their sense of teamwork. When people work on something very hard only to have the supervisor take all the credit, they wonder why they bothered. If you don't share the glory, your employees won't share your enthusiasm for the work.

In order to maintain a sense of teamwork, you have to be accessible and responsive to your people. When they bring you a completed assignment, take time to review it as soon as possible. If it just lies on your desk, they get the message that it wasn't all that important. As soon as you review the assignment, offer feedback. If it meets or exceeds your expectations, show some enthusiasm and encouragement. If your boss or others in the organization will review it, let employees know that you will give them credit for their work. Effective first-line supervisors know that when they share the glory, their people are more committed and eager to take on other tasks. People also have a better sense of teamwork when they know their efforts are properly recognized and rewarded.

Kamile used her twice-a-month department meetings to share success. Employees were given the opportunity to talk about the progress they had made on their goals and assignments. Kamile made a point to recognize their efforts. Sometimes it was with a few words of praise, sometimes she led the rest of the team in a round of applause, other times it was a special certificate of achievement. In many cases she found that it wasn't the actual reward that was important—it was the fact that she had allowed employees to share in the glory of getting a job accomplished.

How have you shared the glory with your team?

_____

_____

_____

✎ Exercise 1: A Group or a Team?

INSTRUCTIONS: Read each situation below and then describe what you would do to improve teamwork.

1. You have been assigned to lead a group made up of people from several different departments. You were told that the group's assignment is to come up with a "Communications Improvement Plan" for the organization. You were given a list of names and told to schedule a meeting to get the ball rolling. The first meeting is scheduled for tomorrow and everyone has responded that they will attend. What would you do at the first meeting?

_____

_____

_____

2. You are a member of a task force that has been asked to come up with a new break room policy that will be implemented companywide when everyone moves into the new headquarters next month. The team has meet once previously and seemed confused about how much authority it had. As a result, they never had really discussed the policy. Instead, they got sidetracked into unrelated issues about the new building. If you were in charge of the team at the next meeting, what would you do?

___

___

___

Suggested Answers
1. First, the group needs to reach agreement on its purpose and goals. Next, they should determine what communication areas they are going to review. Then, they need to develop a plan for gathering and analyzing information so they have a common approach for getting the job done. They also need to make team assignments, so that it is clear who will do what. During the meeting the team should determine if it needs to change the membership of the team so it represents a cross-section of the organization. They should also decide what process to use for reporting results back to the rest of the team.
2. First, you need to find out how much authority and responsibility the team has. Next, find out what is expected of the team so you can determine its purpose and goals. Are they to make policy recommendations or write a specific policy? Once the expectations are clear, keep the team focused on meeting those expectations. Also review the makeup of the team. Perhaps you need to add someone to the group who has experience in writing policy statements. You also should hold members accountable for staying on topic so the task force can meet its objectives.

BEING A VALUABLE TEAM MEMBER

Justin was the weekend supervisor for a retail shoe store that had five locations in one city. He did a good job of making sure things were running well and that customers were being taken care of when he was working. The store manager recognized his ability and asked Justin to be on a task force of supervisors from all the stores to come up with some ideas for improving weekend sales. Justin knew that his store was usually first or second in sales every weekend. He was proud of his accomplishments and didn't want to share his "secrets" with anyone else. He told his manager that he wouldn't have time to participate.

Justin's unwillingness to be part of the task force (team) showed that he didn't understand an important part of being a supervisor—that sometimes he would also have to be a team member. The most effective first-line supervisors know that developing a sense of teamwork means being a good team member themselves. They know they have to hold themselves to the same standards they have for their people.

Justin was short-sighted and didn't see the big picture. Keep in mind that though you may be a supervisor, you are also a member of several teams. First, you are a member of your employees' team, as well as being their supervisor. Second, you are a member of your boss's team. Whether your boss practices all the teamwork skills described thus far, you can demonstrate the benefits of teamwork by how you interact with your supervisor. Third, you may be the member of a team of people drawn from several departments who are working on a specific project. Regardless of which team you are working with, it is your responsibility to be a valuable team member.

✎ Exercise 2: Ten Keys to Being a Valuable Team Member

INSTRUCTIONS: Read each of the statements below. Circle the number that is nearest to how you see yourself, on a scale of 1 to 10, as a team member.

1. I practice "active listening."
   1   2   3   4   5   6   7   8   9   10

2. I promise only what I can deliver.
   1   2   3   4   5   6   7   8   9   10

3. I deliver what I promise, and more.
   1   2   3   4   5   6   7   8   9   10

4. I give credit to others rather than to myself.
   1   2   3   4   5   6   7   8   9   10

5. I seek the contributions of others on a project.
   1   2   3   4   5   6   7   8   9   10

6. I am willing to share my resources with others.
   1   2   3   4   5   6   7   8   9   10

7. I work to resolve conflicts rather than to ignore them.
   1   2   3   4   5   6   7   8   9   10

8. I maintain confidentiality when asked to do so.
   1   2   3   4   5   6   7   8   9   10

9. I maintain a sense of humor even when situations are serious.
   1   2   3   4   5   6   7   8   9   10

10. I smile as often as possible.
    1   2   3   4   5   6   7   8   9   10

Add the numbers you have circled for the ten statements.

Total Score:_____

If you scored:
85 or above: You are likely considered a valuable team member
75–84: You are making some contributions to the team
74 or less: You need to work on developing your teamwork skills
The next section explains how to use these important skills to be a valuable team member.

Use Active Listening

Use your active listening skills to ensure you understand others. Remember to listen for ideas, not just facts, and to control your emotional reactions. Keep an open mind when listening to what others say. Try to understand their point of view.

Listen more than you talk. When you don't understand, ask questions to obtain more information. Test your understanding by paraphrasing and reflecting back what you heard the other person say. You always learn more by listening than you do by talking. When you listen you hear other people's ideas, but when you're talking, you hear only your own.

Avoid Making Commitments You Can't Keep

Don't tell someone you will do something and then fail to deliver. Whether it's your boss, someone in another department, or one of your employees, do what you say you'll do. If you find that you won't be able to meet an agreed to deadline, talk to the other person as soon as possible. Don't wait until the last minute.

Don't take on projects that you know you can't complete. If you can't do something, it's better to say no now than say later you couldn't get the job done. People prefer hearing your honest reaction to being disappointed later when you fail to deliver.

Deliver What You Promise

Keeping your word is an important part of earning the respect and trust of those around you. If your teammates know they can count on you, you'll find yourself being given more substantial responsibilities.

An even better strategy is to deliver more than you promised—and still do it on time. Whenever you exceed expectations, it makes you a more valuable team member. It's like getting dessert free at your favorite restaurant for no apparent reason. You remember those times when you get more than you expected, and the people with whom you work remember your extra effort.

Give Credit to Others

Recognize the contributions of others to your success. There are very few things that you accomplish all by yourself. As noted earlier in this chapter, it's better to acknowledge others. Remember to share the glory with your people; you'll be seen as a more valuable team member.

Seek Contributions of Others

Teams aren't teams unless they work together. When you are faced with a problem, ask other team members for suggestions. Don't wait for them to come to you; they may not know you need help.

When you seek contributions from others, you usually find new ideas and different ways to look at things. You'll also find that other people start coming to you for ideas. By working together, everyone benefits from the experience of other members of the team.

Share Your Resources

Providing support to other team members helps everyone make a more meaningful contribution. Perhaps your area's workload has decreased a bit, whereas another supervisor is swamped. You may be able to provide, at least for a short time, someone from your group to help the other supervisor.

The old saying, "What goes around, comes around," applies here. If you help out another supervisor, you increase the chances that the favor will be returned. The goal is to accomplish as much as possible with the resources available. This means helping each other and not hoarding your resources to the detriment of the organization.

Work to Resolve Workplace Issues

Be willing to openly confront problems knowing that resolving workplace issues can lead to new ideas and greater productivity. Don't let problems or issues build up so they affect the attitude and productivity of your team. The sooner you resolve issues, the better off you are.

Keep Confidences

Resist the urge to use private information to appear valuable, important, or popular with other team members. Respecting all confidences entrusted to you goes a long way to earning the trust and respect of fellow team members.

Being in on the grapevine may seem like a way to be in on life. However, in the long run, you will find better sources of information than gossip and rumors. If you rely on these usually unreliable sources of information, you may find that you get cut off from information about what is really happening.

Maintain a Sense of Humor

A sense of humor can keep minor situations from becoming serious problems. Don't take things too seriously, acting as if there's no tomorrow. To look at some people, you'd think that having fun was incompatible with having a job. Most of us spend more waking hours at work than anywhere else—so why not make it enjoyable?

Having a sense of humor doesn't mean making light of every situation or treating work as a joke. It simply means not treating work as a life and death matter. Keep your perspective and look for the humorous side of things, even if the laugh is on you. Worthwhile work is fun.

Smile

A smile says, "I'm friendly." Team members prefer to work with someone who is happy, and it's hard to get angry with someone who is genuinely happy. A smile helps keep people relaxed and in good spirits. A frown, on the other hand, can make people less open and more tentative in the way they approach their work. You'll be surprised what a difference a smile makes in your own attitude as well as the attitude of those around you.

OBSTACLES TO TEAM DEVELOPMENT

No matter what you do, you'll probably find some people who do not want to be part of a team. Some of their reasons may be valid, others may not. Even with unwilling team members, it is possible to create an effective team by focusing your people on the possibilities of success rather than on their actual or perceived problems. Here is where your skill as a first-line supervisor will be challenged. Exhibit 6–1 describes some of the most common obstacles to team development and provides some suggestions on what you can do to deal with these obstacles.

Your job is to create the right environment, one that allows people to motivate themselves and feel that they are making a contribution. This can mean having individual meetings with people who don't seem to want to be involved. You have to find out why they don't want to be part of the team and address their concerns. Use this opportunity to reaffirm your belief in the team concept and its benefits. This educational process may take some work but, in the end, it is worth it. Adopting the team concept is an impor-

Exhibit 6–1
Obstacles to Team Development

Obstacle	Action(s) You Might Take:
• Too busy with own specific tasks	• Help them develop their time management skills. • Explain the importance of their time as a team member.
• Feel their skills are inadequate and they can't contribute	• Provide training, as needed, to improve skills. • Provide support if they feel inadequate, but reassure them they do possess the needed skills.
• Don't see the need for or benefit of teamwork • Have had a bad experience with teams in the past	• Explain benefits of teamwork and what you want to accomplish. • Describe past successes you have had using teams. • Ask what problems they had in the past, and try to help prevent them.
• Prefer to work alone • Don't like other people on the team	• Explain the benefits of working with others. • Give people a chance to discuss their differences. • Work to resolve conflicts before the team begins work.
• Don't want the bother of being part of a team.	• Describe how team participation is important to organizational success. • Give them an assignment so they can contribute to the team.

...tant step in establishing a climate in which people are inspired to do their very best.

Exercise 3: Removing Obstacles to Team Development

INSTRUCTIONS: Put yourself on the spot for a minute. What do you do that is an obstacle to developing your team? List any obstacle and what action you could take.

I am an obstacle because:

_____

_____

Actions I could take are:

_____

_____

Once you remove your own obstacles, think about the members of your team. Do any of them have obstacles that you might be able to help them remove?

Team Member: _____
Obstacle:

_____

_____

How I could help them:

_____

_____

Team Member: _____
Obstacle:

_____

_____

How I could help them:

_____

_____

© American Management Association. All rights reserved.
http://www.amanet.org/

recap

In this chapter, you learned about the importance and benefits of teamwork. Throughout history, humans have formed groups. Some of these groups became teams when they recognized the resulting benefits.

One definition of a team (a small number of people with complementary skills who are committed to a common purpose, performance goals, and approach for which they hold themselves mutually accountable) was presented and discussed in detail. We also reviewed some specific steps you can take to transform your group into a team.

One of the keys to developing teamwork is to be a good team member yourself. We identified and discussed the ten keys for being a valuable team member. You were asked to rate your own skills on being a team member and were given some guidelines on how to use these skills to be a valuable team member.

Finally, you learned about the obstacles to team development. The reasons why some people do not want to be part of a team were presented along with suggestions on how to deal with their resistance. In the end, your job is to create the right environment that allows people to motivate themselves and to feel they are making a contribution to the team's success.

Exercise 4: Taking It Back to the Workplace

INSTRUCTIONS: Now that you have completed the reading and the activities in this chapter, it's time to think specifically about how to apply what you have learned. The following questions are designed to help you consider what you need to do to succeed back in the workplace.

- What benefits have you experienced from teamwork?
- What actions do you need to take to improve your team's effectiveness?
- How well do you share expectations? Share responsibilities? Share the glory?
- What obstacles are preventing you from having an effective team?
- What is your plan for removing these obstacles?

Review Questions

1. Members of a team tend to:
   (a) recognize their interdependence on others.
   (b) work independently.
   (c) focus on their own goals.
   (d) prefer to have a leader tell them what to do.

   1. (a)

2. Which of the following best describes a team?
   (a) Individuals are asked to share their knowledge and skills.
   (b) Individuals want credit for their own contributions.
   (c) Individuals are cautious about what they say so they won't upset a team member.
   (d) Individuals are willing to do both their own work and someone else's work when the person is absent.

   2. (a)

3. Which of the following is a key to being a valuable team member?
   (a) Making sure your boss is always happy with your work
   (b) Taking credit for work that you do yourself
   (c) Being able to work independently without supervision
   (d) Delivering what you promise on time or early

   3. (d)

4. Sharing the glory is important because:
   (a) most people want the glory all to themselves.
   (b) it lets people know you appreciate their work.
   (c) people expect to get raises for doing their jobs.
   (d) most jobs are harder than the supervisor thinks they are.

   4. (b)

5. The first step in transforming a group into a team is to:
   (a) share the expectations.
   (b) share the responsibilities.
   (c) share the glory.
   (d) remove the obstacles.

   5. (a)

7

Getting the Work Done

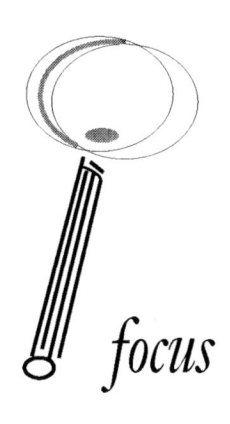

focus

Learning Objectives

By the end of this chapter, you should be able to:

- Identify the factors that affect performance motivation.
- Describe how to obtain top performance from your employees.
- Explain how to use delegation to get work done.
- Identify the procedures for planning and organizing your work.
- Describe how time management and stress affect productivity.

In previous chapters we've discussed the importance of understanding your role and responsibilities, communication, people development, managing people, and teamwork as necessary ingredients to being a successful first-line supervisor. Those ingredients by themselves, however, will not get the work done.

Having all the ingredients for a good dinner is one thing. Being able to put them together to create an enjoyable meal requires a recipe. Just as there are cookbooks for chefs, there are many books available that provide you with "recipes for success" as a first-line supervisor. Whether for cooking or supervision, how well any recipe works depends on the final results: Was the quality acceptable? Unfortunately, in supervision, unlike cooking, all the factors that affect success are not under your control.

To be successful, you have to focus on what you *can* control and avoid worrying about what you *can't* control. In this chapter, we examine some of the factors that affect your success and provide some specific recommendations for actions you can take to increase your chance of success.

Performance Motivation

One of the most common complaints heard from supervisors is, "My people aren't motivated." What these supervisors are saying is that their people don't work as hard, as fast, or as well as the supervisors desire. The fact is, however, that people are motivated. They are motivated to perform at their present level. Their behavior indicates that they perceive their work situation differently from their supervisors. The first thing you need to know is what motivates your employees.

✎ Exercise 1: Job Motivation Factors

INSTRUCTIONS: Below is a list of ten things people want from their work. In the first column, rank order the items from 1 (most important) to 10 (least important) on the basis of how you think the average worker (not supervisor or manager) would rate them. Use the second column to rank order the items in terms of their importance to you as a first-line supervisor.

Importance to:
Workers   You

_____ _____ Feeling of being in on things
_____ _____ Recognition for a job well done
_____ _____ Help with personal problems
_____ _____ Job security
_____ _____ Good pay
_____ _____ Interesting work
_____ _____ Promotion and growth opportunities
_____ _____ Personal loyalty to employees
_____ _____ Good working conditions
_____ _____ Tactful discipline

Suggested Answers
The following is the order most employees rank the items listed.

1. Interesting work
2. Good pay
3. Recognition for a job well done
4. Feeling of being in on things
5. Personal loyalty
6. Job security
7. Help on personal problems
8. Promotion and growth opportunity
9. Good working conditions
10. Tactful discipline

Most employees want their jobs to be interesting. Since many spend nearly half the time they are awake each week at work, they don't want to be bored. Pay is important, and close behind are recognition and being in on things. Compare and contrast your rankings of the two columns. Think about the following questions:

- Do you think most first-line supervisors view things differently from employees? If so, why?
- Do you think you view things differently from your employees? If so, why?
- How do your rankings compare with those in the study?
- How do you think your own employees would rank the items?

You might want to have your employees complete this exercise and discuss it with them in a group meeting. Consider using the following questions for discussion:

- Why did you rank the items in the order you did?
- How can we use this information in our work environment?
- What can I do as your supervisor to create a positive work environment?
- What can you do to create a positive work environment?

The more you learn about what motivates your employees, the more successful you will be in developing a working relationship with them.

Your Role in Motivation

A survey of two million employees at 700 companies by the Gallup Organization in 2000 found that how long employees stay at companies and how productive they are, are determined by their relationship with the immediate supervisor. One of the analysts for the survey summed it up this way, "People join companies and leave managers." This means that the way you treat people and how you respond to them is a major factor in their motivation. As a first-line supervisor you have the most impact on an employee's motivation. The organization provides the pay, the benefits, and other tangibles. It's up to you to provide the intangibles—making work interesting and fun, providing recognition, and the other job motivation factors mentioned earlier—so that employees are motivated.

Different Folks, Different Strokes

Because employees are at various levels of maturity, with individual skills and knowledge, what works with one person may not work with another. In addition, allowances have to be made for different ways of thinking. Human beings are driven by complex internal factors. Though they may react similarly to external motivations, they react differently to those things that affect their internal needs and desires. For example, one person may react positively to increased responsibility, whereas another may prefer the security of the present job.

Some look for independence, others prefer group activities. Some enjoy detailed, structured work; others are motivated by the opportunity to be creative and innovative. All of these motives are invisible to you. Your job is to do your best to analyze people and identify their differences, then use that information to create an environment where people are motivated.

All Behavior Is Motivated

Good behavior as well as bad arises from some motive. Problems occur if you view motivation as a product of only external rewards. Motives are far more complex. To deal with motivational problems, a supervisor must identify every source of negative or positive motivation. One individual may be working too slowly yet be striving for higher quality than someone who works faster. Another may be constantly complaining yet be honestly trying to improve some aspect of the job. The question is not about negative or positive motivation but whether the employees understand the performance the supervisor wants. The solution may be better communication, not greater rewards. Instead of looking immediately for a material source of motivation, a first-line supervisor must analyze all the factors influencing behavior.

First-line supervision is not a popularity contest. A supervisor who wants to be liked may have lower turnover and absenteeism, but the employees may not be motivated to perform better. In fact, you really can't motivate someone else. What you can and must do, however, is to *create an environment where motivation takes place*.

In order to create a motivating environment, you must understand people and their behavior. Everyone has strengths and weaknesses; few are perfect or worthless. Your effectiveness depends on how those strengths are maximized, and how the weaknesses are minimized. Concentrate on specific activities that have a positive effect on behavior.

OBTAINING TOP PERFORMANCE

The performance of your work team is your responsibility; its success is a reflection of your success as a first-line supervisor. Although many first-line supervisors would have you believe that they just can't find good people who are willing to work, there are many other supervisors who, working with similar circumstances, are quite successful. This suggests that the supervisor can make a big difference. If you want to make a difference, you have to apply what you've learned in this course to your specific situation. Here are five approaches to encourage top performance by your employees. All of them have been mentioned previously in other chapters. However, due to their critical nature, they deserve another review.

Establish and Communicate Expectations

Although you shouldn't establish unrealistic expectations, the fact is that most of us can accomplish far more than we do. Both supervisors and workers tend to become satisfied with the way things are. This complacency keeps people and organizations from achieving their full potential. The expectations that you set for your team should cause them to stretch and to achieve more than before. This means being a leader and clearly communicating what you want.

If you don't get the specific results you want, assume that you haven't clearly communicated your expectations. Remember that communication is a two-way process and that you have to accept responsibility for your part. If your team's performance is falling short, the first step is to be sure they understand exactly what you expect. Use all the communication variables you learned in this course—words, voice, and body language—to make your message as clear and direct as possible.

Provide Positive Feedback

Positive feedback should be given when a person consistently meets performance standards, exceeds performance standards, makes a significant contribution, or shows improvement in performance. Make it a habit to look for opportunities to give positive feedback. The 80/20 rule (80 percent positive/20 percent negative) regarding performance should guide your actions.

The positive feedback you provide to your people will strengthen their performance and increase the likelihood that performance will continue to improve. It's especially important to provide positive feedback when people meet the expectations you communicated to them. If you fail to recognize their accomplishments, their performance may slowly go downhill because they assume you don't really care. Maintaining and improving performance is much easier when you provide consistent, positive feedback.

Focus on Teamwork

When your people are part of a team they can accomplish more than they can working as individuals. An effective team enables people to succeed on their own, while recognizing that they are part of something greater. Effective teams are made up of people who seek better ways of doing things. They feel good about themselves and their contributions to the organization.

In any work group, however, there are different styles and approaches, so the potential for disagreement is always present. Disharmony leads to resentment, which exaggerates personality differences; the resulting squabbles can lead people to work at cross-purposes. Therefore, you have to be sensitive to interpersonal relations at all times. The way you handle disagreements can affect the sense of teamwork among your people.

Encourage team members to be accountable to one other and share mutual responsibility for quality performance. Encourage them to learn from each other and use your delegation skills to nudge them into new challenges.

Inspire, but Don't Control

Effective first-line supervisors are committed to achieving their vision. This commitment is revealed in the enthusiasm they have for getting the job done. Such enthusiasm rubs off on people. Trying to control the actions of your people is much less likely to motivate them to meet your expectations.

Inspire your people by helping them understand that increased productivity benefits everyone. Emphasize that higher quality and efficiency increase the amount of control they are given over their day-do-day job responsibilities. No one wants to feel controlled or manipulated, but most of us are willing to be led. As a first-line supervisor this means that once you have communicated expectations and demonstrated your own commitment, you need to get out of the way and let your people work to achieve the goal.

Lead by Example

The example you set for your staff affects their productivity and, therefore, your success as a leader. Even when you are not aware of it, your actions and decisions are being observed and analyzed. In most cases, what you do has a far greater impact on your employees than anything you say. You should be an excellent role model for your people.

You develop loyalty and trust by maintaining high personal standards, by keeping your word, and by being reliable and dependable. Far too many people work in organizations where they do not trust or believe in the messages they receive from their supervisors or their company. As a result, the work is seldom done as carefully and efficiently as possible. Remember, if you want a staff that is honest, loyal, and motivated, you have to be honest, loyal, and motivated yourself.

✎ Exercise 2: What Will I Do?

INSTRUCTIONS: Before you continue with this chapter, take a few minutes to think about some specific things you can do to obtain top performance regarding each of the points just discussed.

1. Establish and Communicate Expectations

   _____

   _____

2. Provide Positive Feedback

   _____

   _____

3. Focus on Teamwork

   _____

   _____

4. Inspire, but Don't Control

   _____

   _____

5. Lead by Example

   _____

   _____

DELEGATING TO GET THE WORK DONE

Byron was overwhelmed. It had been three weeks since he was promoted to first-line supervisor as a member of the operations support team. He had three important projects he was working on when he got promoted. He wanted to make sure they were done right, so he continued to work on them after promotion. He hadn't gotten too much done on any of them because he was so busy learning about his new position and meeting the new people he was working with. He also hadn't expected his boss to give him two more projects at the end of his first week. Now he had five projects to complete, six people to supervise, and log jams in both his e-mail and voice mail. He remembered during the interview that he was told that learning to delegate would be crucial to his success. Now that message was starting to sink in, but Byron was not sure where to start.

Unfortunately, Byron is not alone. Delegation is one of the most important skills for first-line supervisors; at the same time it is often one of the most challenging. The pressures of a new position and the seemingly unending amount of work place a premium on the need to delegate. There is also the tendency to want to "hold on" to some things because you think no one can do it better. Though there may be some truth to that, until you get beyond that kind of thinking the pressure is only going to build. Learning how and when to delegate has several important benefits:

- You are more likely to achieve your goals when you maximize the efforts of your entire staff. Delegation allows you to get others involved in getting the work done.
- Effective delegation allows you to spend your time on your supervisory responsibilities that cannot be delegated to someone else.
- You are better able to manage your own time and focus on your priorities when you delegate to your employees.
- Delegation provides an opportunity for you to develop your people. Delegating allows them to learn new tasks and gives them a chance to be successful. In turn, these new skills may result in their advancement in the organization.

Guidelines for Successful Delegation

Delegation is the process of assigning a project or activity and sharing the responsibility for its outcome (Lane & Rierden, 2001). Successful delegation doesn't just happen. You can't just hand a stack of papers to someone and say, "I need this done as soon as possible." If you want to get work done efficiently and, at the same time, improve your people, you need to follow some basic guidelines. Exhibit 7–1 provides a delegation checklist.

Define the Task to Be Delegated

Be specific regarding what is to be done. Set a deadline for completion and be sure everyone understands what performance is acceptable. When you delegate a task, you should be able to answer some basic questions such as:

Exhibit 7-1
Delegation Checklist

A. Define the task to be delegated
   - Will it take more than one person?
   - How long should it take?
   - What will be evidence of its accomplishment?
   - Will controls be needed along the way?

B. Select the individual
   - How much technical knowledge or experience is needed?
   - Besides your most reliable person, whom could you possibly select?
   - Could this assignment improve someone's skill?
   - What do you want the person to learn from this experience?

C. Delegate the task
   - Tell the person what the assignment is about.
   - Describe exactly what must be accomplished and by what date.
   - Explain why you chose the person and why you feel he or she is capable and dependable.
   - Review the procedure to be followed.
   - Set a final deadline and interim checkpoints.

D. Support the person
   - Define how much support will be needed.
   - Determine what resources you will provide.
   - Avoid reverse delegation.

E. Follow up
   - Recognize work done satisfactorily.
   - Be sure to show your appreciation.

Who will do it? What is to be done? When is it due? Where is the work to be done? How much money is budgeted? Vague instructions lead people to complete tasks that are different from what you expected.

Have a plan for controlling what you assign. The controls should include the deadlines, what is expected, and a series of checkpoints to monitor ongoing progress. The more complicated the assignment, the more checkpoints you may need. As supervisor, you have the ultimate responsibility for the results; but don't overcontrol or undercontrol.

Overcontrol occurs when you are constantly overseeing each detail. This wastes your time and that of the person who is supposed to be doing the task. When you overcontrol, you reduce your employees' initiative and lower their morale. An excessive emphasis on control indicates a lack of trust. The response of your employees will be resentment, anger, and ultimately, apathy.

Undercontrol is more common and even more detrimental. It can lead to unpleasant surprises and incomplete or improperly done assignments. Control is established by having standardized forms, procedures, and deadlines for every delegated task. For many first-line supervisors, this may seem like an unnecessary amount of detail. However, such controls allow everyone to operate from the same set of rules, ensuring consistency from one person to another. Having standards demonstrates your awareness of the different components of a task and clarifies the procedure to follow. When clear standards for getting work done effectively exist, people adhere to those standards.

Select the Individual

Once you know what the task is, you can select the person best suited for the task. Consider how much technical knowledge or experience is needed. Ask yourself: Do I want to use the assignment to develop a person's skill or increase his experience? Or do I want to give this particular task to someone who has the skills and experience because it needs to be done quickly? Each delegation opportunity is different and the person you select depends on both the task and how much development you want to accomplish.

Here are some other factors you may consider when selecting the individual:

- *Motivation and Interest.* Select someone who is self-motivated, has a desire to do the task, and is interested in that type of work. That person is more likely to succeed than someone whom you have to constantly push to get the task done.
- *Respect of Others.* When the task has high visibility and is a high priority, it makes sense to select someone who has earned the respect of others. Such a person will be viewed favorably by the other members of your team who are not selected for the assignment.
- *Willingness to Learn from Mistakes.* When you select someone because you want the experience to be a developmental opportunity, be sure the person can learn from his or her mistakes. Some people are not comfortable taking on a task unless they think they have the necessary knowledge to do it before they start.

Delegate the Task

As a general rule, you should delegate the necessary authority to accomplish a specific task. The person who is responsible for doing the task should also be accountable for its completion. The overall responsibility, however, is yours and should not be delegated. You should not delegate at all when you are specifically responsible for reporting to someone above you—a situation where your input is critical.

Start by giving the person some background so he or she understands what the task is about. Then, describe exactly what must be accomplished. This involves more than telling someone to do something. It means explaining what must be done, why it must be done, and what can happen if it does not get done. The way you describe the task conveys its importance and your confidence in having chosen the best person for the job.

Delegation isn't a one-way street. When people have a voice in what they are to do and how they are to do it, they feel more ownership of the results. Ask those to whom you delegate how much time they think they will need. Often you'll find that people say they can get a job done sooner than you think it can be done. Nevertheless, they have set their own deadline and chances are it will be met. If they come up with a deadline that doesn't meet your needs, you can negotiate a more acceptable one. Be sure the employee knows the procedure to follow, the final deadline, and any interim checkpoints in getting the task completed.

Support the Person
Define the amount of support you'll provide *before* the work starts. Indicate those areas in which you are willing to help, and those for which the employees are responsible. Define precisely the extent of their authority. If you don't do this, they may take on more authority than necessary and involve other employees in the project.

Determine what resources you will provide. These may include time, money, and other people. You may also need to provide copies of materials, checklists, or other items that have been used previously. You may need to let the person know when it is and is not appropriate to come to you. Are there some things they can do on their own and some that they need to check with you before they act? Be sure they understand any limitations you may have.

Effective supervisors insist that their people come to them with solutions to problems, not just problems. Train your people to come to you with their solutions, alternatives, or suggestions when problems occur. Don't take over the work or solve problems for them. If their ideas are not acceptable, give new instructions.

Chances are your employees have some good ideas. If their ideas are acceptable, congratulate them and indicate they should proceed. If they ask for assistance, curb your instinct to reply, "Let me show you how." If you aren't sure about the solution, the tendency may be to say, "Well, let me think about it, and I'll get back to you." When this happens, reverse delegation has taken place, and you wind up doing what you delegated to someone else.

Follow Up
Your success is judged by the results you get. When you delegate control, the results should be as good or even better than if you had done the job yourself. Tell people that you will follow up and then be sure you do. Each time you check back, try to catch them doing something right and then praise them for their efforts.

As mentioned earlier, after a delegated task is completed, share the glory and give credit where credit is due—in front of the entire group whenever possible. Ask those who have done the job, "What would you do differently if given the job again?" Find out what went right and what went wrong. Find out whether they know why some things worked and other didn't. Whenever possible, use their good suggestions and encourage them to apply what they learned on this task to future assignments.

✎ Exercise 3: Preparing to Delegate

INSTRUCTIONS: What tasks are you currently doing that you could delegate, both to reduce your workload and to improve your people? Think about an assignment that you currently have that you could delegate. Use the worksheet below to prepare the assignment for delegation.

1. What specific task do you want done?

   _____
   _____

2. To whom should you delegate the task?

   _____
   _____

3. How will you control the assignment?

   _____
   _____

4. What support will you provide?

   _____
   _____

5. How will you follow up?

   _____
   _____

PLANNING AND ORGANIZING FOR SUCCESS

Few first-line supervisors adequately address the need for planning in their daily, weekly, or monthly activities. It's easy to fall in the trap of focusing immediate concerns or becoming a problem solver or "firefighter." However, solving other people's problems for them and jumping from one task to another is no substitute for planning. Such an approach, in fact, is usually the result of *not* planning.

Planning is a management process designed to produce results. A well-thought-out, organized plan helps you monitor your daily efforts and verify that you are moving in the right direction to achieve your goals and those of the organization.

Although your plan describes numerous activities that need to be done, don't confuse activity with results. Just because you are busy and working a lot of hours doesn't mean that you are doing what needs to be done. In fact, an effective plan can enable you to work fewer hours yet accomplish more by doing the right things at the right times.

Exhibit 7-2
Elements of a Successful Plan

Measure what is being done now.
- Identify your exact responsibilities: production, service, profits, units, quality, etc.
- How does your company measure your performance?

Develop data or other objective measures to determine the following:
- Your team's performance relative to previous periods
- Your team's performance relative to existing goals

Determine which job components you can control, for example:
- The number of employees you supervise
- The specific tasks they do

Analyze what you will need from others.
- Identify the forms of cooperation or coordination needed.
- Identify the resources needed or available.

Develop a plan by asking these questions:
- Where am I today?
- Where do I want to go?
- How will I get there?
- How am I doing?

Exhibit 7–2 outlines five steps you should employ when developing a plan. These include developing data to measure performance, identifying those areas or activities over which you have control, and identifying the resources and cooperation you need to fulfill your plan.

You may feel your only responsibility is to get the work out. Regardless of the complexity or simplicity of your work, however, you should never come to work with no better plan than just to handle the problems as they occur. Depending on the length of your work cycle, you should always have a plan for tomorrow, the next week, or the next month.

Imperatives of Planning

Planning doesn't prevent the unexpected from happening. However, research has shown that it does help accomplish what is expected. Back in the 1950s, a behavioral research team at Harvard Business School chose 100 members of the senior class and asked them what they would like to be doing ten years after graduation. All 100 said they would like to be wealthy, successful, and significant forces in the business world. The researchers noted that only ten of the students had put their goals in writing.

Ten years later the research team visited the 100 students to see what had been accomplished. They found that the ten students who had written their goals had 96 percent of the total wealth of the 100-student sample. Those ten students met their own expectations in part because they had a plan (Sherman, 1991).

Make Your Plan Specific, Achievable, and Measurable

Develop plans that specify those results you desire and those you will accept. Determine what objective proof will confirm your success. Determine what procedures can be improved and to what degree. Merely wanting things to be better or hoping they will improve doesn't cut it.

Whatever your plan, it has to be judged by you and your team as achievable and worthwhile. Just because you think you have a great plan, doesn't mean your team will work feverishly to help you fulfill it. Whenever possible, involve your team in the development of your plan; they'll be more likely to help you make it work.

Plans Should Be in Writing

Written plans help eliminate, or at least reduce, the possibility of different interpretations. Plans based on memory tend to become fuzzy over time. Written plans also enable your people to measure the extent of your commitment and their role in the process. Remember the Harvard students mentioned earlier—those who put their plans in writing were far more successful than the ones who did not. Written plans facilitate analysis of each step in the process, and provide a structure on which to base future planning. It's also much easier to review plan results when you have something in writing from the outset.

Plans Must Have a Timetable

Having a timetable with intermediate deadlines prevents your team members from procrastinating. In some situations, you may want to establish weekly or even daily goals. Avoid making plans so long range or indefinite that people lose interest. As each step is achieved, be sure all the people involved are kept abreast of individual and team progress. Determine the long-range impact on other departments as well as on your own team.

Determine Priorities Beforehand

Almost every task comprises a sequence of events—some things have to be done before others. Your plan should reflect this sequence. Knowing what comes first and what is most important allows people to prepare themselves. In addition, having your priorities established ahead of time helps everyone avoid sudden changes and readjustments. It also helps you determine where in the plan to fit in some new concern or procedure.

Communicate What Is Going On

Be sure you obtain commitments for any necessary assistance from your peers and consent, if needed, from your boss before finalizing your plan. They can help you expedite the plan and offer suggestions on how to improve it. Share with them your vision of the benefits and opportunities that will result if your plan succeeds.

Exhibit 7-3
Milestone Chart

Action Required	Team Member(s) Responsible	Week of May 3	Week of May 10	Week of May 17	Week of May 24
Outline approved	Ron and Sue	◆			
Prepare first draft	Margaret and Bill		◆		
First draft review	Content experts			◆	
Revisions/final draft	Margaret and Bill				◆

Use the sample Milestone Chart as a template to develop your own. You may need to use legal-size paper and a landscape format if your project takes several weeks.

Keep in mind that your plans must be compatible with those of the organization. Consider the impact on other areas, and make sure that what it achieves supports the goals of the entire organization, not just your own area of responsibility.

One of the tools you can use to develop a written plan is called a *milestone chart* (see Exhibit 7–3). A milestone chart shows the key steps in a plan and when they are to be completed. Assigning specific responsibility for certain steps adds accountability to the planning process. Milestone charts are easy to develop and easy to review. They enable you to see at a glance what progress has been made, what remains to be done, and whether people are meeting their deadlines.

Expect Some Obstacles and Disagreements
You may not get all the necessary resources you need—time, money, or people. Be prepared to ask for assistance from people in a position to help you. If you can't obtain all the resources you need, be prepared to develop an alternative plan within the constraints of the resources you have.

Set Up a Review Process
Your plan has to be flexible so it can be adjusted when circumstances change. Allow for the unexpected, and be prepared to make quick adjustments whenever necessary to keep your plan on track.

Questions Your Plan Should Answer

Every element discussed so far is essential for a workable plan. As you construct your plan, you need to answer four overriding questions. Exhibit 7–4 shows the relationship among those questions. Notice that they form a continuing cycle.

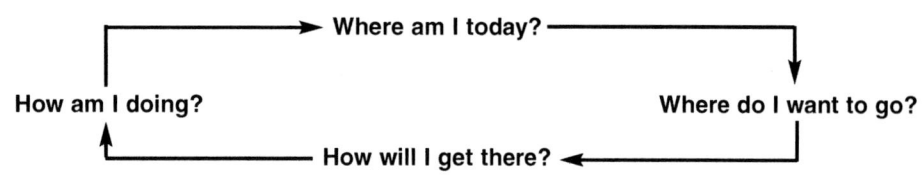

Exhibit 7-4
Planning Cycle

```
        ┌──→ Where am I today? ──┐
        │                        ↓
How am I doing?           Where do I want to go?
        ↑                        │
        └── How will I get there? ←┘
```

Where Am I Today?

First, you have to know where you are today. Begin by identifying current strengths as well as opportunities for improvement. Ask yourself questions such as: What am I doing that works well? What current activities should I continue doing? What could I do to take advantage of these strengths? What improvements need to be made? What opportunities exist to improve productivity? The answers to these questions combine to answer the larger question, "Where am I today?"

Where Do I Want to Go?

When Alice was in Wonderland and found herself at the fork in the road, she asked the Cheshire Cat which path to take. The cat asked her where she wanted to go. Alice replied that she didn't know. Said the cat, "If you don't know where you're going, any road will lead you there." Until you can clearly define what it is you want to accomplish, any plan will be okay. The problem is you may wind up somewhere that you don't want to be. After examining your strengths and areas of opportunity, you have to define where it is you want to go. What results do you want your team to achieve? How might things be different if you implement a plan? Only when you know where you want to go are you ready to decide which road to take.

How Will I Get There?

Now you're ready to plan the specific actions. Questions to ask at this point include: What programs or strategies will help me get where I want to do? Who can help me achieve the desired results? What resources do I need to make the plan a reality? What deadlines need to be established? As before, the more specific you can be, the better you'll be able to measure your results.

As you put together your plan, it's important to establish priorities. Determine what needs to be done first, second, third, and so on. Unless you establish priorities, you may find yourself and your team working on things unrelated to your plan. Soon you fall back into the firefighting mode without time to accomplish the important goals you identified during the planning process.

How Am I Doing?

Once the plan is written and you've started to implement your plan, the next step is to evaluate how you are doing in meeting the plan's objectives.

Questions you want to ask include: Am I on track? Am I achieving the expected results? Do changes need to be made? At this point the cycle begins again as you make necessary adjustments to your plan. You may determine that some portions of the plan are no longer valid or that some items need to be added to make your plan more workable.

Some first-line supervisors have trouble with this step. They have a tendency to stick with the original plan, no matter what happens. Changes to the plan are threats to their ego or authority. The reality is just the opposite. Those who fail to be flexible often wind up headed in the wrong direction. They may accomplish their original goals, but they contribute nothing to the success of the organization.

As a first-line supervisor you have to be flexible, just like a good football coach who enters the game with a definite plan. If the other team quickly scores two or three touchdowns, the coach makes adjustments to the plan. He knows that if he sticks to the original plan, things will continue to get worse and his team could lose the game. Being willing and able to modify the game plan can be the difference between success and failure, whether you are a coach or a first-line supervisor.

✎ Exercise 4: Developing Your Plan

INSTRUCTIONS: Now it's your turn. Use the process just described to develop your own work plan to improve one area of your responsibility for the next month, quarter, six months, or year. If you are new at developing plans, you may want to start with a smaller time frame, such as a month. Later you can expand the plan to cover a longer time frame.

Name: _____

Department: _____

Area of focus: _____

Plan time frame: _____

  I. Where am I today? (Consider strengths, weaknesses, and opportunities)

_____

_____

_____

 II. Where do I want to go? (What will be different when my plan succeeds?)

_____

_____

_____

III. How will I get there? (What programs or strategies do I need?)

_____

_____

_____

IV. How am I doing? (How will I measure my success?)

_____

_____

_____

Managing Your Time

In striving to make your plan work, one of your most valuable resources is time. Like money, it must be spent wisely. Many people and tasks will require your time and attention. You will be tempted to respond to them immediately. However, the more often you respond to things that aren't part of your plan or priorities, the more often you'll find yourself not accomplishing what you set out to do.

Time management has been the subject of many books, training films, and seminars. There are a number of time management systems on the market (Day Timer, Day Runner, and Franklin Covey are a few of the popular ones). They come in all shapes, sizes, colors, and costs. Each has its devoted band of users, who wouldn't think of trying any other system. In the end, however, the important thing is to have a system that works for you, which may not be the same system everyone else is using.

You may be able to use nothing more than a simple calendar as a time management tool. If you don't currently have a system you may want to try out various systems to find the one that works best in your situation. Here are a few time management hints you can apply regardless of the system you use.

Use a Daily List of Things to Do

Set aside a few minutes each day to list things you need to get done. Some people like to do this first thing in the morning; others prefer to do it at the end of the day, so they can get right to work the next day. Putting tasks in writing increases the likelihood that they'll get done (remember the Harvard study).

Prioritize Your Daily List

Unless you prioritize your daily activities, you may find yourself very busy but not getting very much accomplished. Most time management experts recommend that you use three categories: (1) Must be done, (2) Should be done, and (3) Nice to do. Some suggest further prioritizing by breaking down each of these categories (1a, 2a, 3a, etc.). Unless you set priorities there is a temptation to work on the 3s (they often are the easiest or take the least amount of time) and not get to the 1s and 2s.

Determine the Best Use of Your Time Right Now

Several times each day, you should ask yourself: What would be the best use of my time right now? If you are working down your list of priorities, the answer to this question should keep you focused on what must be done rather than what should be done or what would be nice to do. It's also a good question to ask whenever you are offered a new obligation or when another priority gets added to your list. Despite your best intentions, it's easy to get off track and start working on something that doesn't have a high priority.

Manage Your Time Like Money

Keep track of what you use and balance your time like you would balance a checkbook. Determine how much time you are spending on various parts of your plan. Are you spending more time on what should be done than on what must be done? Each day do you accomplish something that must be done? Do you waste time by not having a daily list of things to do?

Try this exercise for one week. Use the Daily Time Log in Exhibit 7–5 to keep track of how you spend your time at work each day. At the end of the week, add up the time you spent on all the different things you did. Put a dollar figure on each item based on your hourly rate (if you're on salary, divide your weekly salary by the average number of hours you work each week). You'll be able to see, on a weekly basis, what your organization is paying you for each of your activities. Then ask yourself: If it were my company, would I think I got a good return on my investment? Your answer to this question can help you determine if you are managing your time wisely or whether time is managing you.

Strive for Life Balance with Your Time

Some people say that the term time management should really be referred to as event management, because what we really are doing is managing the events in our lives. Too many people get caught up in managing the events at work without doing anything to manage the events of their lives outside of work. Chances are you already find yourself pulled in many directions. In addition to work responsibilities, you most likely have one or more of the following competing for your time: family commitments, community involvement, school activities, church activities, and professional organizations. The result of these competing factors can be stress, which affects your responses and your response time. So how do we manage all the events in our lives?

Author and consultant, Stephen Covey, in his best-selling book, *The 7 Habits of Highly Effective People* (1989), offers several suggestions. When dealing with time management, Covey says that there are four generations of time management, which he refers to as quadrants:

Exhibit 7–5
Daily Time Log

NAME: _____ DATE: _____

Time	Task	Cost
7:00–7:30		
7:30–8:00		
8:00–8:30		
8:30–9:00		
9:00–9:30		
9:30–10:00		
10:00–10:30		
10:30–11:00		
11:00–11:30		
11:30–12:00		
12:00–12:30		
12:30–1:00		
1:00–1:30		
1:30–2:00		
2:00–2:30		
2:30–3:00		
3:00–3:30		
3:30–4:00		
4:00–4:30		
4:30–5:00		
5:00–5:30		
5:30–6:00		

Quadrant I: Important and Urgent
Quadrant II: Important, Not Urgent
Quadrant III: Not Important, Urgent
Quadrant IV: Not Important, Not Urgent

He suggests that people should put first things first by spending more time in Quadrant II. If we do that, Covey says we become more principle-centered and manage ourselves to do what is truly important. In order to fully understand and appreciate his concepts, take time to read his book. This thumbnail sketch barely scratches the surface of what he has to say. The key point is that each of us has more control over how our time is spent, but we must be willing to take control rather than letting time (events) control us.

© American Management Association. All rights reserved.
http://www.amanet.org/

Effects of Stress on Productivity

Today's hectic work schedules and our personal and family needs all contribute to stress. But it is not always true that stress is bad. Some people handle stress quite well. Many athletes, for example, often do their best when the pressure is greatest. Some stress is valuable. Any real challenge entails stress, which is part of the exhilaration of a challenge and part of the satisfaction of success.

As a first-line supervisor, you are definitely subject to stress in your day-to-day work. There are people problems, production problems, and your own personal problems. The secret of handling stress lies in how you react to it, and how you deal with your fellow workers.

Stress that has no redeeming value can arise from uncertainty and lack of control. Such stress also occurs when supervisors use threats, intimidation, or excessive force to dominate the work group. All of these sources of stress lead to a decline in performance and productivity. Your ability to create a clear and workable plan and explain it to your employees helps reduce stress and maintain a positive work environment.

It's important that you keep your perspective in every situation and keep your people from overreacting to events that seem beyond their control. Many first-line supervisors allow stress to build up unnecessarily in the workplace. They feel that the work, their boss, or the company is causing the stress, and they communicate this attitude to their work groups. Note the word "feel," because stress is largely determined by our subjective interpretation of the circumstances: Stress does not arise from a situation itself but from our attitude toward it.

Often, stress is an inappropriate response to a situation. It's important to maintain open and honest communication with your employees so you know what they are thinking and feeling about their work and your expectations. For example, if your company were facing possible lay-offs, your employees would feel stress, which might be severe enough to undermine morale and productivity. You would have to level with them about how you are feeling and keep them informed about what's really happening. Otherwise, what they hear through the grapevine may create even more stress. When you keep your employees informed, you have a greater chance to minimize stress.

recap

This chapter focused on several factors that affect you and your team's ability to get the work done. First, we discussed performance motivation. There are many motivational variables, some of which are beyond the control of the first-line supervisor. We learned, though, that all behavior is motivated in some way and that different people have different motivational needs. Your job as a supervisor is to determine what motivates your employees and then create an environment where they can motivate themselves.

Second, we looked at how getting the work done requires that you get top performance from the members of your team. Top performance is the result of establishing and communicating expectations, providing positive feedback, focusing on teamwork, inspiring your people rather than controlling them, and leading by example.

You also learned about the benefits and importance of delegation. A five-step process for effective delegation was presented: defining the task to be delegated, selecting the individual, delegating the task, supporting the person, and following up.

The importance of planning was presented along with guidelines for developing an effective plan: make it specific, achievable, and measurable; put it in writing; have a timetable; determine priorities; and communicate the plan. The use of milestone charts was also discussed. The best plans answer the questions: Where am I today? Where do I want to go? How will I get there? and How am I doing?

Finally, the crucial nature of time management was discussed. We suggested ways to more effectively manage your time, such as using a daily to do list, prioritizing the list, determining the best use of your time at any given moment, and managing your time like money. Guidelines were also presented for how to balance life events with work events.

Exercise 5: Taking it Back to the Workplace

INSTRUCTIONS: Now that you have completed the reading and the activities in this chapter, it's time to think specifically about how to apply what you have learned. The following questions are designed to help you consider what you need to do to succeed back in the workplace.

- ❏ Do you know what motivates the members of your team?
- ❏ What have you done to encourage and obtain top performance?
- ❏ How effective have you been at delegating tasks?
- ❏ What tasks are you doing that you should be delegating?
- ❏ How much time do you spend planning and organizing? Do you need to be spend more or less time? Why?
- ❏ What improvements do you need to more effectively manage your time?

Review Questions

1. How do you apply the 80/20 rule when giving feedback to employees about their performance?
   (a) Keep a log so that you make sure 80 percent of what you say is positive.
   (b) Avoid giving negative feedback at least one day a week.
   (c) Every time you give negative feedback, try to give some positive feedback at the same time.
   (d) Make it habit to look for opportunities to give positive feedback.

   1. (d)

2. When establishing expectations, it is important to set standards that:
   (a) can easily be met so morale will be high.
   (b) are slightly higher than last year.
   (c) challenge and stretch people's abilities.
   (d) are the same as similar work groups in your organization.

   2. (c)

3. Which of the following is *most* true when delegating a task?
   (a) Controls should have deadlines and checkpoints.
   (b) Controls should be tight or things will go wrong.
   (c) Controls should be open to indicate your trust.
   (d) Controls are unnecessary for simple, repetitive tasks.

   3. (a)

4. The best reason for having a plan is that:
   (a) it tells management you are cooperative.
   (b) it helps reduce "firefighting."
   (c) if anything goes wrong, you can determine who was at fault.
   (d) you never have to deal with unexpected events.

   4. (b)

5. Which of the following best describes the role of stress?
   (a) Stress is bad and should be avoided.
   (b) Stress causes ulcers and heart attacks.
   (c) Some stress is positive and valuable.
   (d) Stress is reduced when supervisory control is reduced.

   5. (c)

© American Management Association. All rights reserved.
http://www.amanet.org/

8

Supervising in a Changing Environment

Learning Objectives

By the end of this chapter, you should be able to:

- Identify legal issues that impact first-line supervisors.
- Explain your role in supervising a diverse workforce.
- Explain the concepts of virtual work and distance management.
- Describe the first-line supervisor's role in managing change.

The speed of change in today's world is amazing. New technologies designed to make our work and personal lives easier and more productive seem to be introduced almost daily. At least that's what we're told. For some, these constant changes create more stress and some become less productive because they have so many things to do they can't seem to get any one of them done. Some people long for the good old days, when getting something delivered overnight was fast enough. Now we need that e-mail attachment or downloadable file immediately, because tomorrow is too late. As a first-line supervisor you are likely to find that patience among those you work for and with is an old-fashioned virtue. People want it yesterday and oftentimes they don't seem to care how you get it done as long as you meet their deadline.

This chapter deals with some of the changes in the work environment that affect the way you do your job. Because of the constant nature of change you won't find a lot of definitive answers, but you will find some guidelines that should help you supervise in a changing environment.

LEGAL ISSUES FOR FIRST-LINE SUPERVISORS

Rich had a dentist appointment the first thing Tuesday morning. While he was in the waiting area, he checked his office e-mail and found a message from Kasandra, the company's director of human resources. She had just received a call from an attorney who represented Shelia Lewis, whom Rich had terminated two weeks ago for not meeting his expectations. The attorney said they were considering filing a lawsuit charging Rich and the company with "constructive discharge." Kasandra wanted to know what Rich did to Shelia. He wasn't sure how to respond because he had never heard the term before. How about you? Do you know what it is? If not, you're probably not alone. It's another example of the changes taking place in today's work environment.

Constructive discharge is a legal concept that employees sometimes use to sue their former employers. They claim that conditions at work had become so intolerable that any reasonable person would have quit. It doesn't matter whether you fired her or she eventually quit. If the court rules the circumstances a constructive discharge, you're just as liable. Such things as moving a person to an undesirable work area, giving them undesirable tasks, or making them work at undesirable times could all come under scrutiny. This is just one example of the many changes that you may have to deal with as a first-line supervisor. Though you don't have to have a law degree, you do need to have some awareness of the laws that impact you and some techniques to protect yourself and your company.

Government Laws and Organization Policies

Hundreds of federal laws pertain to employee rights. They are designed to prevent discrimination and ensure equal employment opportunity. Exhibit 8–1 shows just a few of the most important laws that impact the workplace. Many cities and states have laws that are more comprehensive and restrictive than federal legislation. These laws vary by state. If your organization has a legal department or retains legal counsel, check with them regarding legislation that affects you. If you don't have access to legal resources, the Department of Labor (at the federal level and in many states as well) can provide assistance.

Most organizations also have their own policies and procedures tied to these federal and state laws. One of the best things you can do is to become familiar with the expectations of your organization. Generally, if you comply with your organization's policies you should be in compliance with any similar federal and state requirements. As a first-line supervisor you also need to be sure your employees are knowledgeable because their actions, good and bad, reflect back on you.

Another important consideration for many organizations is safety. Companies must adhere to numerous environmental and occupational laws. Some companies have a safety director or risk management department that formulates policies and procedures. Again, it is your responsibility to understand these policies and ensure your employees follow them.

Exhibit 8-1
Federal Legislation in the Workplace

The laws summarized here are not intended to be a comprehensive list. Consult with your organization's legal counsel or human resources department for information on how they affect you.

1. *Title VII of the Civil Rights Act of 1964 (amended and renamed Equal Employment Opportunity in 1972)*
   Prohibits discrimination on the basis race, color, religion, sex, marital status, or national origin.
2. *Age Discrimination in Employment Act*
   Protects certain applicants and employees 40 years of age and older from discrimination on the basis of age in hiring, promotion, discharge, compensation, or terms, condition, or privileges of employment.
3. *Americans with Disabilities Act (ADA)*
   Prohibits discrimination against people with disabilities in employment, transportation, public accommodation, communications, and government activities.
4. *Fair Labor Standards Act (amended by the Equal Pay Act)*
   Sets federal minimum wage standards as well as the requirements for overtime pay. If an employee works in a state that has its own minimum wage law the employee is entitled to the higher wage.
5. *Family and Medical Leave Act (FMLA)*
   Employers with more than fifty employees must grant eligible employees up to a total of twelve workweeks of unpaid leave during any twelve-month period. Reasons for leave includes the birth and care of a newborn child, adoption or foster care, care for an immediate family member, or medical leave for a serious health condition.
6. *Immigration and Nationality Act (Amended and renamed Reform and Control Act)*
   Prohibits employers from hiring illegal aliens. Provides guidelines for employment of aliens in the United States and requires workers to produce legal documents to prove that they have permission to work in this country.

For more information about these and related laws, go to www.dol.gov.

Avoiding Legal Action

In sports they often say that the best offense is a good defense. In the legal arena that is definitely the case. But don't just think in terms of avoidance or being on the defensive. In many cases the laws with which you have to comply were passed because organizations didn't treat people right in the first place. Organizations that treat people right because it is the right thing to do typically have few legal issues to deal with. Their actions are based on what is a fair and equitable way to treat their employees.

Here are some practices to help you *prevent* the need for others to take legal action. If they do, however, these practices will also prove valuable.

- *Document your actions.* Make sure you document your interactions with employees. Good records are helpful in discussing employee performance. They are also valuable should you be faced with a prospective day in court.
- *Train your employees.* The best way to make sure employees know what is expected is to train them to do their jobs. Organizations that fail to train

open themselves up to problems when they fire employees for non-performance. Be sure you document the training as well.
- *Treat people consistently.* Do your best to treat everyone the same. The more consistent you are, the less likely you are to have problems.
- *Don't say bad things about ex-employees.* When a person leaves for whatever reason, make it a point to say only good things, or to say nothing at all. Negative comments to others always seem to work their way back to the person being talked about.
- *Rate people fairly.* When doing performance evaluations make sure your ratings are fair and equitable. Don't give people ratings that are higher or lower than they deserve. In the event of legal action about how you rated one person you may be asked to explain how you rated others.
- *Consult with Human Resources.* Don't try and do everything on your own. Talk to your HR department about situations you are unsure about how to handle. If you don't have such a department, consult legal counsel.

Exercise 1: Legal Issues Scavenger Hunt

INSTRUCTIONS: This activity will help you learn about how your organization addresses the more common legal issues. For each item, identify the source of information and then set aside time to review the information.

Legal Issue	Source of Information	Reviewed
Equal Employment Opportunity		
Age Discrimination		
Hiring and Job Offers		
Employees with Disabilities		
Medical Leave		
Sexual Harassment		
Violence in the Workplace		
Safety Policies		
Employee Compensation		
Overtime Pay		
Disciplinary Procedures		
Termination Procedures		
Other		
Other		

SUPERVISING A DIVERSE WORKFORCE

Diversity comes in many forms—the most obvious is in people. The federal government's *Workforce 2000* study found that today's workforce is no longer the province of white males. In fact, white males make up only 43 percent of the workforce and by 2005 the study projected that white males would represent less than 15 percent of those entering the workforce. Though they still represent a sizeable number of those in supervisory positions, women and other so-called minorities, such as Afro-Americans, Asians, Pacific Islanders, and Hispanics, are becoming more evident in leadership roles in many organizations.

At PepsiCo, CEO Steve Reinemund has said that if the company is to achieve its goals it has to replicate within the organization the demographics of its consumers. That means making a commitment to increasing the ethnic and cultural diversity of its senior management team. For all organizations there will likely be a continuing increase in the diversity of both their total workforce and those in supervisory positions. Successful organizations look at this as a beneficial trend and use it to their advantage.

Your Role in Supervising Diversity

Diversity means more than just the color of one's skin, race, or gender. There is also diversity that comes with differences in age, assertiveness, personality type, disabilities, and even in the way people process information and ideas. How you handle each type of diversity and possible resulting situations depends on the circumstances. Though it is impossible to address all those variables in this course, here are some general guidelines for supervising a diverse workforce.

Be a Role Model
You can't just pay lip service to diversity; you have to walk the talk. This means speaking up when people say negative things about others. If you remain silent when someone disparages another person or group, your silence is interpreted as agreement. Being a role model also means confronting incidents that run counter to diversity. You have to let people know that their actions are both counterproductive and unacceptable. Your employees, peers, and upper management should be able to tell by both your words and your actions that you place a value on diversity.

Understand and Respect Individual Differences
Not everyone sees things the way you do. That doesn't make them wrong, only different. As a newspaper editor once told me, "If we both agree on everything, there's not a need for both of us." Be willing to accept that others view things differently than you do. Don't automatically try to win someone over to your point of view. Sometimes the best course of action is to agree to disagree.

Learn How Others Want to Be Treated
Don't assume that your way is the right way. If you are unsure of how a person pronounces her name or whether she wants to go by a nickname, ask. Some people, depending on cultural differences, may not want a real pat on the back or react negatively to verbal praise in public. Have empathy for the other person. Put yourself in his or her shoes and think about how you feel when someone treats you differently than you want to be treated. Find out how people want to be treated and do your best to treat them that way.

Take a Stand

This is the flip side of the above. Let people know how you want to be treated. Don't be afraid to speak up if someone else's words or actions offend you. Even if someone says something that isn't directed at you personally, but it offends you, tell him or her your point of view. Also, if someone tells you that something you said or did offended him, don't get defensive or angry. Be glad the person was willing to share and then make sure you correct the situation in the future. Honesty and openness goes a long way in creating an environment where people respect and value each other's diversity.

Be Open to Differences

Diversity of people naturally leads to diversity of thought and perspective. Situations and problems that once seemed to have clear-cut answers are now being challenged by people with different points of view. Many people are more willing to share their own insights than before. The best supervisors openly solicit these more diverse viewpoints because they realize that they are able to make better-informed decisions. If you ignore the diverse viewpoints of your employees, you do so at your own peril.

Exhibit 8–2
Developing Your Diversity Awareness

Here are some things you can do to increase your awareness of the diversity that is all around you. There is also space for you to list some ideas of your own.

- Think before you speak.
- Be sensitive to others and to their point of view.
- Practice active listening.
- Be tactful when talking to others.
- Respect others and their individuality.
- Pay attention to the whole person; not just what's different.
- Be aware of your own biases and prejudices.
- Avoid stereotypes and generalizations.
- Ask people questions to find out about them.
- Learn about other cultures and lifestyles.
- Be aware of your own "blind spots."
- Maintain a sense of humor when things go wrong.
- Avoid trying to make others think like you do.
- Don't put people on the spot because of their beliefs.

- _____
- _____
- _____

Developing Yourself for Diversity

The guidelines in the previous section can be applied to different types of situations that you face as a supervisor. There are also several things that you can do personally to develop your own appreciation and understanding of diversity in your organization. Exhibit 8–2 provides some examples. There is also room for you to add your own ideas. The more you learn and the more you know, the better able you will be to value the diversity that affects your both your work life and your personal life.

✎ Exercise 2: Analyze the Diversity of Your Organization

INSTRUCTIONS: Answer the questions below to analyze the diversity of your organization and your work team.

Yes   No

____ ____   1. We have a diverse workforce in terms of age.

____ ____   2. We have a diverse workforce in terms of gender.

____ ____   3. We have a diverse workforce in terms of race.

____ ____   4. We have a diverse workforce in terms of personality types.

____ ____   5. We have a diverse workforce in terms of how people think.

____ ____   6. We have a workplace that accommodates and accepts people with disabilities.

____ ____   7. We view diversity as a positive factor.

____ ____   8. We actively recruit people who will help us have a diverse workforce.

____ ____   9. Our diversity is obvious to those outside our organization.

____ ____   10. My feelings about diversity are the same as those in upper management.

Look back at the items you answered "no" and list some things you might do as a first-line supervisor to make changes.

_____

_____

_____

The Distance Manager and Virtual Work

Roberto had been a salesperson for his company's line of office products for the past five years. His wife was recently offered a promotion with her company that would require them to relocate within the state, but about 250 miles from their current location. Rob liked working for his company and didn't want to resign. He had heard about people working out of virtual offices and working at remote locations. He also knew a couple of salespeople at other companies who were working from their homes instead of at the company's headquarters. He decided to talk to his supervisor, Karissa, to see if she would buy into the idea. She too had heard about the concept and said she had been thinking about giving it a try. They both agreed that maybe this would be a good time to test the concept. Little did Karissa or Roberto know what was waiting for them as they embarked on this new effort.

How is being a distance manager different from what you do currently? It has been described this way: "In some ways being a distance manager is like trying to be a leader with your hands tied behind your back while you're wearing a paper bag over your head" (Fisher and Fisher, 2001). Although this may be somewhat of an exaggeration, it is certain that being a distance manager is not the same thing as being a manager where everyone who works for you is on-site with you, or "co-located" to use the distance management terminology.

The purpose of this section is to introduce you to some of the concepts and considerations that you should be familiar with regarding distance management and virtual work. The ultimate decision about using these concepts will most likely be made by those in higher management positions. Being aware of some of the basics, however, can help prepare you in the event your organization chooses to organize some or all of its work in this manner.

What, Why, and When of Distance Management and Virtual Work

A *distance manager* is someone who is responsible for managing people who are not located at the same place at the same time. One example would be a sales manager who works at the company headquarters and has a staff of salespeople who work out of separate offices located in different cities. Or it could be project manager who is coordinating the work of several people, some of whom may not even be employees of the company, who are located in various places around the country. The possibilities are almost limitless.

Virtual work is what the people who are located away from the manager, do. People are able to work virtually thanks to e-mail, fax machines, laptops, Internet access, cell phones, Web or video conferencing, networks, and the continually emerging technologies that allow people to "connect" with each other regardless of where they are located.

It has been estimated that 95 percent of the *Fortune* 1000 companies have implemented virtual work (Hoefling, 2003), often in the form of telecommuting. More and more companies are moving in this direction. Some of the primary reasons are:

- *Reduced Overhead.* Companies can often save money by having people work from home or in office space that is less expensive than building or moving to large office space. There is also a potential for savings in travel costs because people can hook up for such things as Web conferences rather than traveling to a face-to-face meeting.
- *Reduced Labor Costs.* Some organizations make use of contract employees who are not included in benefit programs and other types of compensation, such as bonuses, that are given to regular employees.
- *More Productive Employees.* Studies have shown that people actually can get more done in less time when they have more control over their working environment. There are fewer interruptions and distractions than in a typical workplace.
- *Recruiting and Retention.* Roberto's situation described at the beginning of this section is becoming more commonplace. Organizations want to keep valuable, experienced employees and not lose them because a spouse has to relocate. Virtual work also allows people more choices in terms of work/life balance that is so important in today's society.
- *Getting Closer to the Customer.* Having people working at remote locations also allows more frequent personal contact with customers. Oftentimes people who are located off-site can get to their customers quicker than if they had to travel from the home office.

The uses of distance management and virtual work are limited only by the imagination. Opportunities abound for organizations that are willing to make the leap away from the traditional ways that work has been organized. But to be successful, it requires more than just a few people who are willing to give it a try. Perhaps the most important factor is the culture of an organization. The way an organization views and values such things as independence, control, collaboration, and worker competence affects the success of virtual work. In other words, the organization can't just talk about it—it has to support the concept with action. If you become involved in the process you have to be willing to make the commitment and follow through to see that it works. It is also critical that workers receive the resources, training, and support they need to be successful in their new roles.

Being a Successful Distance Manager

The good news is that the competencies required to be a successful distance manager are the same as those required of all effective managers. Here are the seven competencies (Fisher and Fisher, 2001) that are needed:

1. Articulate a vision for the organization.
2. Get good results.
3. Actively facilitate and develop team members.
4. Aggressively eliminate barriers to team effectiveness.
5. Understand and communicate business and customer needs.

6. Effectively coach individuals and teams.
7. Set a personal example.

All of these have been discussed in detail elsewhere in this course. The bad news is that they are often more difficult to do from a distance. When you don't see people face-to-face, the interpersonal exchanges become much harder. For example, coaching someone when you can't see his or her body language or make direct eye contact becomes even more difficult. Conversely, think how tough it can be to set a personal example when people can't see you. As a first-line supervisor there is a tendency to want to control what people are doing. The distance manager, on the other hand, has to teach people to control themselves because he or she can't be there to exert day-to-day control.

If you find yourself becoming a distance manager be sure you ask for and receive some training specifically geared to your new responsibilities. Find out what is expected of you and your virtual employees. You can use the skills you have learned in this course as your base, but you need to learn to apply them in your new environment.

Being a Successful Virtual Worker

Not everyone is cut out to be a virtual worker. Some people start out liking it, but find that they miss such things as the social aspects or working with others. In the end, they want to go back to a regular work setting. Other people thrive in an environment where they have more control over when they work, how they work, and the way they dress for work. Let's look at some of the things to consider if you are called upon to select people to work at remote locations.

- *Technical Competence.* People have to be comfortable working with technology. They have to have a good understanding of computer hardware and software. They have to know how to use e-mail, download files, share files, access networks. Although they don't have to be technology gurus, they have to know enough so that the supervisor doesn't have to spend an inordinate amount time solving technical problems.
- *Communication Skills.* With less face-to-face communication and more one-way communication, people must be able to express themselves clearly. They also have to be good listeners as they are often on the receiving end of communication that cannot be repeated without slowing down others in the virtual loop.
- *Good Judgment.* People working independently have to make many decisions on their own. They often won't have the time or the opportunity to check with someone else—instead they have to rely on what they think is best. Making the wrong decisions not only affects that person's work, but also can have a significant impact on the work of others.
- *Time Management and Organization.* Virtual workers must coordinate activities with others and have the self-discipline and self-motivation to get their own work done. They have to be able to organize their workspace

and find things when needed. They have to get themselves to work on time and make sure they maintain their productivity during the day.
- *Being Comfortable Working in Isolation.* Water cooler conversations, coffee breaks with colleagues, lunch with other employees, and regular social contacts are nonexistent for the virtual worker. Some workers find such isolation their greatest obstacle. The missing social aspect of work leads to lower productivity and unhappiness on the job.
- *Willingness to Be Accountable for Results.* Virtual workers don't have anyone else to "blame" when something goes wrong. They have to accept responsibility for their decisions. They can't have a "victim" mentality. Effective virtual workers like to take the initiative to get things done rather than waiting for someone else to do something.
- *Being Adaptable and Flexible.* Change in the virtual world is a certainty. A willingness to embrace new technology, new demands, and new ways of doing things is critical. What worked today may not work tomorrow. Someone may want to try something different next week to see how it works. Plans and schedules can change with little notice. People who want structure and continuity have trouble adapting to virtual work.

Organization Success Factors

No matter how skilled you are as a distance supervisor or how carefully you select virtual workers, several factors determine whether your organization is likely to succeed in adopting this style of work. Exhibit 8–3 lists some of

---

Exhibit 8–3
Dos and Don'ts for Implementing Virtual Work

Here are several things that can affect the likely success of making the transition to successful implementation of virtual work.

Dos
- Make sure the organization culture is supportive.
- Have a plan for sharing good ideas so people aren't reinventing the wheel.
- Clearly communicate expectations.
- Have a kick-off meeting to explain everything to everyone involved before they start.
- Make sure the technology is available and that it works.
- Make sure the right people are selected for both management and worker positions.
- Be prepared for some bumps along the way.

Don'ts
- Start a "pilot program" to see whether it will work here; it can be viewed as another management fad. Instead do a "pilot program" to determine how to make it work *in our organization.*
- Limit people's access to new tools and technologies.
- Give up if it doesn't work immediately.
- Be autocratic; allow people input into their work and decisions.
- Abdicate decision-making; be involved in the decision-making process.

the dos and don'ts for organizations that are considering using distance managers and virtual work. Although you may not have a great deal to say about some of these things, being aware of them enables you to ask pertinent questions and helps you ensure your organization focuses on the right things.

✎ Exercise 3: Will It Work Here?

INSTRUCTIONS: Take a moment to think about what you just read. Also consider your own knowledge and experience with virtual work. Answer the questions that follow to give yourself some perspective on how you view these important considerations:

Would you like to be distance manger? If yes, what will it take to prepare you to succeed?

_____

_____

Would you like to be a virtual worker? If yes, explain why.

_____

Who are some people you think would make good virtual workers?

_____

_____

_____

How many virtual workers does your organization have now?

_____

What do they do?

_____

How many virtual workers are planned for in the future?

_____

What will they do?

_____

_____

What changes, if any, does your organization need to make to be more successful with its virtual work efforts?

_____

_____

MANAGING CHANGE

In today's fast-paced world, change is continual. No sooner is one change made than another one comes along to take its place. And sometimes multiple changes are thrust on you all at once. As a first-line supervisor you may have only limited control over the number and type of changes you face. Many changes are likely to be decided higher up the management ladder, and your job is to see that the changes are implemented. It's important then that you understand a little bit about the nature of change and your role and responsibilities in implementing change.

Stages of Change

Most people don't like change. They get comfortable with the way things are, and they like the predictability. Even when we know the change is for the better, we still tend to resist. Given the choice between doing something again like we did it yesterday or changing the procedure, most opt for doing the familiar—even if logic tells us otherwise. Experts who have studied the change process have identified several stages that people go through when faced with change. Although they may disagree on what they *call* the individual stages, there is general agreement on four stages, which we'll refer to as:

1. Denial
2. Resistance
3. Adjustment
4. Involvement

Denial

When a major change is announced, the first reaction is often numbness. People hear it, but they don't accept it. They don't believe it will really happen. They may even seem apathetic to the whole idea, as if ignoring it will make it go away. You get a new boss, and your initial reaction may be, "I won't change, so it really won't make any difference. I'll just keep on doing what I'm doing." During the denial stage, we often pretend the change won't affect us unless we let it. Or, if the change does happen, it will be over real soon.

Resistance
Once people realize the change is going to happen, their feelings most likely change to anger, anxiety, frustration, self-doubt, or uncertainty. During this time, people may become negative in what they say. People who are normally happy at work, now find things that make them unhappy. Morale drops, along with productivity, as people realize the change is really going to happen. They may begin to lose sleep, withdraw into themselves, or even try to think of ways to combat the change. This is usually the low point for most people as they evaluate the situation and try to decide what to do.

Adjustment
Once they accept the change, people begin to make adjustments to what they believe the future will be. They begin to start thinking about what might happen and how they can have an impact. A lot of ideas may be generated, and some enthusiasm for the change may be evident. At the same time, there is often a lack of focus. Chaos may even result because people try to think of every possible scenario and how they should respond. Frustration can result when people realize they have lots to do, but aren't really sure where to start.

Involvement
As the first three stages wind up and things begin to become clearer, people are willing to embrace the change. They find ways to make a contribution and a commitment to the change. They begin to have a sense of satisfaction with the change. Not only do they like the change, they may even wonder what all the fuss was about when they first heard about the change. You know that the change has been accepted when people seem to be satisfied with way things are working and they feel like part of a team.

Managing Change as a First-Line Supervisor

As mentioned earlier, your primary role is to implement changes someone else in the organization has deemed appropriate. Initially, you will probably experience, to one degree or another, each of the four stages of change. Going through the change mentally yourself, while at the same time having to lead its implementation in your work group, can be extremely challenging. Before you throw yourself into the change management process, you may want to read some other books and articles on the subject. One source of useful information is the AMA Self-Study course, *Planning and Managing Change* by Vivette Payne.

Exhibit 8–4 provides a very basic description of your role in managing change. It is similar, but not identical, to what you find in other texts on the subject. Consider it as a starting place as you begin to assume responsibility for managing change within your organization.

✎ Exercise 4: Thinking About Change

INSTRUCTIONS: Take a moment now to think about an upcoming change that you have to help implement. Answer the questions below to help you with your planning.

What upcoming change will directly affect you and your work team?

_____

_____

What can you do to prepare for the change?

_____

_____

_____

What can you do to execute the change?

_____

_____

_____

What can you do to follow up after the change?

_____

_____

_____

_____

Exhibit 8–4

Role of the First-Line Supervisor in Managing Change

I. Prepare for the Change
   A. Understand the change yourself.
   B. Find out what will *not* change.
   C. Set goals for the change.
   D. Develop a plan for introducing the change.

II. Execute the Change
   A. Introduce the change to employees.
   B. Deal with resistance to change.
   C. Expect problems, but be prepared to deal with them.
   D. Be available to help employees with the change process.

III. Follow-Up to the Change
   A. Maintain open communication with employees. Ask, "How's it going?" or "How can I help?"
   B. Troubleshoot problems and provide solutions/ideas.
   C. Provide positive reinforcement when change occurs.
   D. Keep working to make the change permanent.

recap

This chapter began with a discussion of legal issues that can impact a first-line supervisor. You learned about some of the federal laws that specify what you can and cannot do. You were encouraged to become familiar with the expectations of your organization by learning its policies and procedures. You were also given several practices that can help you prevent the need for others to take legal action.

Then, you learned about the value and benefits of having a diverse workforce. You were given several guidelines for supervising a diverse workforce as well as some suggestions of things you can do to develop your own diversity awareness.

You were introduced the concepts of being a distance manager and virtual work. You learned that although the competencies are similar to those of first-line supervisors, distance managers have to approach their responsibilities differently. Some of the considerations for selecting virtual workers were discussed along with some of the factors that can affect an organization's success when implementing virtual work.

Finally, we looked at managing change. You learned that when people experience a change, they typically go through four stages: denial, resistance, adjustment, and involvement. Their actions and reactions vary depending on which stage they are experiencing. You also looked at a process a first-line supervisor can use for managing change and applied that to a current situation.

Exercise 5: Taking It Back to the Workplace

INSTRUCTIONS: Now that you have completed the reading and the activities in this chapter, it's time to think specifically about how to apply what you have learned. The following questions are designed to help you consider what you need to do to succeed back in the workplace.

- ❑ What, if any, legal issues do you need to address?
- ❑ Do you know whom to consult if you have a legal question?
- ❑ How do you interact with those who are different from you?
- ❑ How much value do you place on diversity?
- ❑ What opportunities are there for virtual work in your organization?
- ❑ How will distance management and virtual work affect you in the next six months? In the next twelve months?
- ❑ What change initiatives are coming up?
- ❑ What have you done to prepare for the change?

Review Questions

1. Which of the following legislation addresses the issue of religion as it relates to hiring?
   (a) Family Medical Leave Act
   (b) Americans with Disabilities Act
   (c) Equal Employment Opportunity
   (d) Wage and Hour Laws

   1. (c)

2. Which of the following would be the best way to show that you value diversity?
   (a) Establishing quotas for hiring and promoting employees
   (b) Trying to learn as many foreign languages as possible
   (c) Trying to imitate the way other people act and talk
   (d) Learning how others want to be treated and treating them that way

   2. (d)

3. A good distance manager:
   (a) uses the same skills as any other first-line supervisor.
   (b) builds on the skills learned as a first-line supervisor.
   (c) requires virtual workers to report in every day.
   (d) maintains a great deal of control over the work being done.

   3. (b)

4. The *best* candidate to be a virtual worker would be someone who:
   (a) is a self-starter.
   (b) likes frequent contact with others.
   (c) has never been a virtual worker in the past.
   (d) has limited technical expertise.

   4. (a)

5. During which change stage is an employee most likely to have a lot of ideas, but still lack focus?
   (a) Denial
   (b) Resistance
   (c) Adjustment
   (d) Involvement

   5. (c)

9

Ensuring Your Success

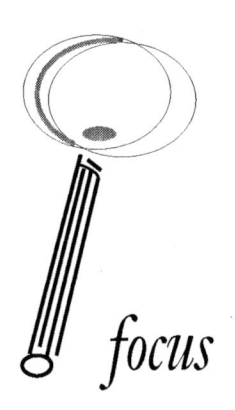

focus

Learning Objectives

By the end of this chapter, you should be able to:

- Reevaluate your confidence in making the transition from employee to first-line supervisor.
- Identify your skill areas that need additional development.
- Prepare a personal action plan for your first ninety days as a supervisor.
- Set goals for your ongoing professional development.

While reading and completing the exercises in this book you may have, at times, felt overwhelmed at how much there is to learn and what is expected of you. As you assume your new responsibilities, you will find that being a first-line supervisor is never boring: Every day you are likely to be faced with new problems to solve and new challenges to meet.

Regardless of how you feel right now, you can have a direct impact on your success by applying what you have learned. Research has shown that when people do not act on new learning within a few months, much of the learning tends to be lost. This chapter gives you the opportunity to review what you have learned, to build on your knowledge and skills, and to develop a plan to be successful.

REEVALUATE YOUR CONFIDENCE LEVEL

Let's start at the beginning. In the first chapter you completed a self-assessment of your confidence level in making the transition from employee to first-line supervisor. Now that you have completed the first eight chapters, it's time to reevaluate your confidence level. Your confidence level should have increased as your knowledge has increased. You have also had numerous opportunities throughout the course to think about ways to apply what you have been learning. This too, should have increased your confidence in making a smooth transition. The ten items in the exercise that follows are identical to the exercise you completed in Chapter 1. However, don't look back at your earlier responses. This time you'll be using the results to help develop a plan for your first ninety days as a first-line supervisor.

✎ Exericse 1: My Confidence Level

INSTRUCTIONS: Read each of the statements below. Circle the number that is nearest to your confidence level on a scale of 1 to 10 (with 1 being "Not Confident" and 10 being "Very Confident") in being able to make the transition from employee to first-line supervisor.

1. I can shift the focus from my area of technical or functional expertise to supervising other people.
   1   2   3   4   5   6   7   8   9   10

2. I can make the transition from being a doer to ensuring work gets done.
   1   2   3   4   5   6   7   8   9   10

3. I can handle multiple priorities at one time.
   1   2   3   4   5   6   7   8   9   10

4. I can shift my focus from my job and my department to become aware of the entire organization and the role of individual departments and the relationships among departments.
   1   2   3   4   5   6   7   8   9   10

5. I can shift my focus from the quality of my own performance to the quality and performance of the entire team.
   1   2   3   4   5   6   7   8   9   10

6. I can handle working the extra hours that may be required in my new role.
   1   2   3   4   5   6   7   8   9   10

7. I can make the transition from being an information receiver to being an information provider.
   1   2   3   4   5   6   7   8   9   10

8. I can make the transition from being concerned about my own personal satisfaction to a concern for motivating and developing my employees.
   1   2   3   4   5   6   7   8   9   10

9. I can make the transition from being a team member to being a team builder.
   1   2   3   4   5   6   7   8   9   10

10. I can maintain a positive attitude when more demands are placed on me.
    1   2   3   4   5   6   7   8   9   10

Evaluation

Refer to the Action Plan in Exhibit 9–1. Use Section A to identify those areas that you rated as 7 or less. These are items that require additional development during your first ninety days so you can make a successful transition to first-line supervision.

Set goals for yourself beginning in the Action Required column. Be as specific as possible in stating your goal. A sample is provided for your reference. Next, determine what *additional resources* you may need, such as reading a book, attending a seminar, subscribing to a magazine, etc. Then identify what *additional support* you may need. Support might come from your boss, a peer, a mentor, etc. In order to keep on track, set a *target date* for completing each goal.

Note: Keep your plan realistic. Do not set more than two goals in Section A to work on during the first ninety days. If you have more than two items you rated as 7 or less, prioritize the top two.

ADDITIONAL SKILL DEVELOPMENT

The higher your confidence level, the more likely you are to succeed as a first-line supervisor. In addition to confidence, you also must have the skills necessary to lead your team. The exercise that follows allows you to evaluate your skill level. The items in the exercise are based on the content of Chapters 3 through 8.

✎ Exercise 2: My Skill Areas

INSTRUCTIONS: Review each Skill Area below. If you need to refresh your memory regarding the specific skills, refer back to that chapter in the book. Then write in the number that is nearest to your skill level on a scale of 1 to 10 (with 1 being "Not Skilled" and 10 being "Very Skilled"). Rate yourself on each bulleted skill area, not the overall category.

Chapter Reference	Skill Area	Skill Level
3	*Communicating* • Listening • Planning and Conducting Meetings • Written Communication • Communication Technology	_____ _____ _____ _____

Chapter Reference	Skill Area	Skill Level
4	*Developing People* • New Employee Orientation • Employee Training • Coaching Employees	_____ _____ _____
5	*Managing People* • Providing Performance Feedback • Working with Difficult Employees • Managing Workplace Conflict • Taking Disciplinary Action	_____ _____ _____ _____
6	*Building a Team* • Transforming a Group to a Team • Being a Valuable Team Member • Dealing with Obstacles	_____ _____ _____
7	*Getting Work Done* • Performance Motivation • Obtaining Top Performance • Delegating • Planning and Organizing • Time Management	_____ _____ _____ _____ _____
8	*Supervising in a Changing Environment* • Legal Issues • Managing a Diverse Workforce • Managing Virtual Employees at Distant Locations • Managing Change	_____ _____ _____ _____

Evaluation

Refer to the Action Plan in Exhibit 9–1. Use Section B to identify those areas that you rated as 7 or less. These are skill areas that require additional development during the first ninety days.

Set goals for yourself beginning in the Action Required column. Be as specific as possible in stating your goal. A sample is provided for your reference. Next, determine what *additional resources* you may need, such as reading a book, attending a seminar, or subscribing to a magazine, etc. Then identify what *additional support* you may need. Support might come from your boss, a peer, or a mentor. In order to keep on track, set a *target date* for completing each goal.

Note: Keep your plan realistic. Do not set more than three goals in Section B to work on during the first ninety days. If you have more than three items you rated as 7 or less, prioritize the top three. Your total number of goals in both A and B should not exceed five. If you have more than

E Exhibit 9–1
Action Plan for My First Ninety Days

New First-Line SupervisorImmediate Supervisor

_____
Date Started

Section A: Confidence Level

Score	Item

Action Required	Additional Resources	Additional Support	Target Date
Be able to handle multiple priorities	Outside seminar	Meet with boss to develop plan	6/10/xx

Section B: Skill Areas

Score	Item

Action Required	Additional Resources	Additional Support	Target Date
Balance work and personal life	Read *The 7 Habits of Highly Effective People*	Discuss with assigned mentor	07/20/xx

© American Management Association. All rights reserved.
http://www.amanet.org/

five solid goals for your first ninety days you are probably not being realistic and are setting yourself up for failure.

You now have an Action Plan for your first ninety days in position. Take the initiative to schedule a meeting with your immediate supervisor to discuss your plan at the outset. Ask for additional recommendations, guidance, and support in making your plan realistic and meaningful. Then, keep your Action Plan where you can easily access it during your first ninety days in position. Review it weekly to be sure you are making the necessary progress in achieving your goals. If you get off track, make appropriate adjustments and review the plan again with your immediate supervisor.

Ongoing Professional Development

The frequency with which you pursue formal ongoing professional development will vary. It is recommended that you begin by completing a review after your first ninety days on the job. The timing of your next review depends on how you and your immediate supervisor feel about your development at that point. You may want your next follow-up plan to be for three months, six months, or a year. The timing may also depend on any organizational requirements for performance review and action plan development.

An important source for ongoing development is coaching and guidance from your immediate supervisor. If he or she provides you with regular feedback, be thankful. Many people receive only limited feedback from their bosses and what they do receive tends to be negative. If you aren't getting feedback from above, take the bull by the horns yourself. Go to your boss and ask for help. But do so only if you really want help. Remember the saying, "Be careful what you ask for—you just might get it." An experienced and successful boss, however, can be an excellent source for your own personal development.

Your peer group can be another place to go for ongoing development. Look around and find out which first-line supervisors are successful. Ask them to explain what they have found that works well for them. It may not work 100 percent for you, but some of what they do may be applicable. Peers are likely to have similar problems and experiences to yours. Their insight can be valuable as you develop your own knowledge, skills, and abilities.

Don't forget your employees and team members. If you interact with them on a daily basis, they probably know you better than anyone else. Use team meetings to ask for input and suggestions on ways to improve. If you are open about wanting their participation in your development, they will willingly provide you with feedback about your performance.

The evaluation and goal setting process described in this chapter should be an ongoing developmental activity. Personal growth occurs when you take time to ask hard questions about how you are doing, listen to the responses, and then make a concerted effort to improve performance. Over time this continual process of feedback and evaluation leads to professional growth and the development of important leadership skills.

recap

This chapter was designed to provide you with an opportunity to prepare yourself for your first ninety days on the job as a first-line supervisor. You were asked to make an assessment of your confidence level and your skills areas. Based on your assessment you developed an action plan with specific goals for your first ninety days.

You were also challenged to make evaluation and goal setting an ongoing professional development activity. It was pointed out that personal growth occurs when you take time to obtain serious feedback from others and then make a concentrated effort to improve your own performance. This continual process of feedback and evaluation can keep you headed in the right direction and help you achieve your long-term goals.

Review Questions

1. Why is it important to do an assessment of your confidence and skills before becoming a first-line supervisor?
   (a) It allows your boss an opportunity to evaluate you.
   (b) It provides you with a rationale for poor performance.
   (c) It helps you identify areas for continued development.
   (d) Other supervisors can compare their results with yours.

   1. (c)

2. An action plan for the first ninety days should include a total of no more than ____ goals.
   (a) two
   (b) three
   (c) four
   (d) five

   2. (d)

3. Attending an outside seminar is an example of:
   (a) something every new first-line supervisor should do.
   (b) an additional resource used to develop your skills.
   (c) a learning experience you attend with your new boss.
   (d) an experience that would benefit few supervisors.

   3. (b)

4. The *best* source for identifying your ongoing development needs would be your:
   (a) immediate supervisor.
   (b) peer group.
   (c) employees and team members.
   (d) immediate family.

   4. (a)

5. Ongoing professional development is important because it:
   (a) provides documentation of past performance for legal purposes.
   (b) gives your immediate supervisor information for your performance appraisal.
   (c) helps keep you on track for achieving your professional goals.
   (d) reduces the amount of time required when making promotion decisions.

   5. (c)

Bibliography

Bock, Wally. *Getting on the Information Superhighway* (Los Altos, California: Crisp Publications, 1996.)
This book provides a starting point for learning about and using the information superhighway.

Broadwell, Martin M. *The New Supervisor*, 2nd Ed. (Menlo Park, California: Addison-Wesley, 1984.)
This book covers the basic techniques of supervision and management. It includes practical advice on delegation, communication, planning, directing, and training.

Cadwell, Charles M. *Developing an Employee Orientation and Training Program* (Boston: American Management Association, 1990.)
This audiocassette/workbook program takes you step-by-step through the process of developing effective employee orientation and training systems that meet organizational needs and improve employee relations.

Cadwell, Charles M. *The Human Touch Performance Appraisal* (West Des Moines, Iowa: American Media Incorporated, 1994.)
This book focuses on the process of conducting performance appraisals, not the paperwork or "form." The process described helps managers build on their employees' strengths so they can reach their true potential.

Chapman, Elwood N. *Supervising Part-Time Employees: A Guide to Better Productivity* (Menlo Park, California: Crisp Publications, 1994.
The author discusses the use of a part-time workforce and the management considerations that are necessary to make it work.

Covey, Stephen R. *The 7 Habits of Highly Effective People* (New York: Simon & Schuster, 1989.)

This best-selling book presents a holistic, integrated, and principle-centered approach for solving personal and professional problems. The seven habits provide a guide for taking charge of one's work and personal life.

Davis, Jeffrey H. *Coaching for Top Performance* (Watertown, Massachusetts: The American Management Association, 1995.)
This self-study program helps the reader discover how skillful coaching can turn ordinary employees into top performers. The focus is on working with your people and how to effectively support their efforts.

Drucker, Peter F. *Management* (New York: Harper & Row, 1973.)
Considered to be a landmark study of management as an organized body of knowledge. It not only deals with the techniques of effective management, but also looks at management from the outside and studies its tasks and requirements.

duPont, Kay, CSP. *Handling Diversity in the Workplace: Communication Is the Key* (West Des Moines, Iowa: American Media Incorporated, 1997.)
This book is intended to help readers understand how their words and actions in today's diverse workplace affect their organization's bottom line, and why everyone needs to maintain and exhibit a positive outlook on diversity.

Fisher, Kimball and Maureen Duncan Fisher. *The Distance Manager* (New York: McGraw-Hill, 2001.)
The authors draw on the experience of a cross-section of managers who have been placed in the challenging world of distance managment and have done the job well. They provide numerous tips for managing from a distance.

Hall, Robert W. *Attaining Manufacturing Excellence* (New York: Dow-Jones-Irwin, 1987.)
This book provides a one-stop source for understanding such important management concepts as Just-In-Time, Total Quality Management, and Continuous Improvement.

Hoefling, Trina. *Working Virtually* (Sterling, Virginia: Stylus Publishing, 2003.)
The author provides guidance through work charts, composite examples, definitions, and actual cases for those who manage and work with dispersed workforces.

Jones, John E., Ph.D. and William L. Bearley, Ed.D. *360° Feedback: Strategies, Tactics, and Techniques for Developing Leaders* (Amherst, Mass.: HRD Press, 1996.)

This practical handbook spells out how the emerging technology of multi-source assessment and feedback can benefit all types of organizations.

Katzenbach, Jon R. and Douglas K. Smith. *The Wisdom of Teams: Creating High-Performance Organizations* (New York: Harper Business, 1994.)
This book offers valuable advice on the fine art of building teams for high performance results. It contains numerous examples, recommendations, and useful ideas for making teams work.

Lane, Byron and Richard Rierdan. *Managing People*, 4th Ed. (Central Point, Oregon: The Oasis Press/PSI Research, 2001.)
The authors discuss several essential business skills including strategic thinking, motivating, adapting to change, setting goals, coping with stress, and empowering a team.

Maddux, Robert B. *Team Building: An Exercise in Leadership*, Rev. Ed. (Los Altos, California: Crisp Publications, Inc., 1992.)
The author provides the principles and methods needed to develop successful problem-solving teams. He also teaches the concepts that help transform a group into a team and provides guidance on how to make work positive and productive.

Mager, Robert F. *What Every Manager Should Know About Training* (Belmont, California: Lake Publishing Co., 1992.)
A jargon-free book that helps managers use training and other performance tools to get top performance from employees. The author reveals common myths about training and shows how to tell whether a training program is good, bad, or even necessary.

Maslow, Abraham H. *Motivation and Personality*, 2nd Ed. (New York: Harper and Row, 1970.)
The author explains how one's personality and one's motivation are two interrelated factors that, when combined, help determine a person's success in life.

Micale, Frances A. *Not Another Meeting! A Practical Guide for Facilitating Effective Meetings* (Central Point, Oregon: The Oasis Press/PSI Research, 2002.)
The author stresses the importance of creating an agenda, proper opening and closing of meetings, establishing ground rules, involving all participants, handling group conflict, and working with difficult individuals.

Payne, Vivette with Wendi Gedzun. *First-Level Leadership: Supervising in the New Organization* (Watertown, Massachusetts: American Management Association, 1998.)

Designed for the first-level supervisor confronting the task of providing leadership in a dynamic business environment. Teaches the concepts and skills needed to manage the "new" workforce, influence others, and create and foster organizational stewardship.

Peters, Thomas J. *Thriving on Chaos* (New York: Alfred A. Knopf, 1986.)
The author challenges what we think we know about managing and often challenges our basic American management traditions. He provides advice on how to manage business in a turbulent and rapidly changing business climate.

Rye, David. *Attracting & Rewarding Outstanding Employees* (Santa Monica, California: Entrepreneur Press, 2002.)
The author talks about how to spot outstanding employees and future stars, how to get the most from your outstanding employees, and how to sell a candidate on your company.

Shea, Gordon F. *Managing Older Workers: Overcoming Myths and Stereotypes* (Menlo Park, Calif.: Crisp Publications, 1994.)
The author discusses how effective management policies and practices can encourage older employees to remain in the workforce longer and become even more productive in their jobs.

Sherman, James R., Ph.D. *Plan Your Work: Work Your Plan* (Los Altos, California: Crisp Publications, 1991.)
This book provides some simple and easily followed techniques that will help the reader become more productive by developing a plan and then working that plan.

Simons, George F. *Working Together: How to Become More Effective in a Multicultural Organization* (Menlo Park, California: Crisp Publications, 1989.)
The author provides three broad steps to follow: manage your mind, manage your words, and manage your unspoken language as the keys to understanding and respecting people of other cultures and being understood and respected by them.

Stevens-Long, Judith and Michael L. Commons. *Adult Life: Developmental Processes*, 4th Ed. (Mountain View, California: Mayfield Publishing, 1992.)
This comprehensive introduction to adult development and aging offers a balanced treatment of the early, middle, and late adult development stages.

Tepper, Bruce B. *The New Supervisor: Skills for Success* (West Des Moines, Iowa: American Media Incorporated, 1995.)

The author covers the skills needed to think like a leader, gain respect and support, ensure tasks are accomplished on time, and encourage team building.

Watkins, Michael. *The First 90 Days* (Boston, Massachusetts: Harvard Business School Press, 2003.)
The author provides his roadmap for taking charge quickly and effectively during critical transition periods, whether a person is a first-time manager or a new CEO.

Weiss, Donald. *How to Be a Successful Manager* (New York: AMACOM, 1986.)
This short guide provides suggestions for creating a productive work environment, handling grievances and difficult employees, troubleshooting problems, and making decisions more quickly.

Post-Test

First-Line Supervision
Fifth Edition

Course Code 90029

INSTRUCTIONS: *To take this test and have it graded, please email AMASelfStudy@amanet.org. You will receive an email back with details on taking your test and getting your grade.*

FOR QUESTIONS AND COMMENTS: *You can also contact Self Study at 1-800-225-3215 or visit the website at www.amaselfstudy.org*

pp. 30-31
1. When working with your boss it is best to:
   (a) tell your employees everything your boss tells you.
   (b) develop a partnership with clear expectations.
   (c) assume 50 percent of the responsibility for the relationship.
   (d) develop a relationship with your boss's boss.

p. 5
2. When dealing with information, a first-line supervisor has to act as a(n) _____ between employees and upper management.
   (a) interpreter
   (b) insolation
   (c) gatekeeper

(d) motivator

p.10
3. Part of the paradox of first-line supervision is explained by which of the following statements?
   (a) Supervisors are expected to get employees to work more hours.
   (b) Supervisors only have limited authority over employees.
   (c) Supervisors should not expect to make many decisions.
   (d) Supervisors need to be competent despite limited training.

p.14
4. Which factors do effective supervisors consider when choosing the most appropriate leadership style?
   (a) Availability, quality, experience
   (b) Availability, quality, time
   (c) Experience, time, information
   (d) Experience, information, quality

p.169
5. One of the primary reasons for companies to implement virtual work is to:
   (a) reduce overhead expenses.
   (b) reduce training costs.
   (c) outsource more work overseas.
   (d) reduce the need for supervision.

p.22
6. Because employees look to their supervisors for structure and direction, a first-line supervisor should:
   (a) handle problems and issues.
   (b) provide resources.
   (c) plan and organize work.
   (d) focus on administrative tasks.

p.53
7. The best way to develop your own listening habits is to:
   (a) stop the speaker as soon as something isn't clear.
   (b) hear the person out, and don't interrupt.
   (c) compare what is being said with what you already know.
   (d) be thinking of questions for the speaker.

p.112
8. The conflict management style that seeks the best for both parties is:
   (a) collaboration.
   (b) compromise.
   (c) avoidance.
   (d) accommodation.

p.75
9. The best orientation programs:
   (a) are completed the first day on the job.
   (b) involve the employee in planning the orientation.
   (c) ensure policy manuals are ready prior to beginning a task.
   (d) are developed and implemented by line management.

POST-TEST 195

p.91 **10.** When coaching an employee whose performance has slipped, the first step is to:
(a) tell the person how to improve.
(b) get the person to tell you when improvement will be made.
(c) wait until the person comes to you and asks for help.
((d)) get the employee to agree performance needs improvement.

p.64 **11.** Electronic messaging is best used for:
(a) communicating confidential information.
((b)) normal day-to-day communication.
(c) setting the stage for disciplinary action.
(d) saying things you wouldn't say face-to-face.

p.108 **12.** When working with difficult employees it is best to focus on the employee's:
(a) attitude.
(b) attendance.
((c)) behavior.
(d) home situation.

p.101 **13.** In order for employee feedback to be effective it should:
((a)) be specific and immediate.
(b) focus on the negative first, the positive second.
(c) be used sparingly so employees don't expect to get it.
(d) be put in writing and a copy placed in the employee's file.

p.87 **14.** One thing you can do to make sure the training that your employees attend is effective is to:
(a) have them pay for the training themselves.
(b) send several people at one time.
(c) have them attend on weekends or on days off.
((d)) recognize their improvement after the training.

p.174 **15.** The adjustment stage of the change process is frequently characterized by feelings of:
(a) anger and numbness.
(b) self-doubt and uncertainty.
(c) contribution and commitment.
((d)) chaos and frustration.

p.148 **16.** Which of the following is characteristic of reverse delegation?
(a) The supervisor reverses a bad decision when a problem occurs.
((b)) The supervisor winds up doing the work that was delegated.
(c) The supervisor is able to identify resources that are needed.
(d) The supervisor can select the best person to do a task.

© American Management Association. All rights reserved.
http://www.amanet.org/

17. Which of the following can be an obstacle to team development? [p.134]
    (a) Being too busy with your own tasks ✓
    (b) Delegating too many tasks
    (c) Asking employees for input too often
    (d) Spending too much time coaching employees

18. Which of the following is the <u>best</u> thing you can do to help avoid legal action by employees? [p.164]
    (a) Spend time learning the details of employment law.
    (b) Consult with legal counsel before taking disciplinary action. ✓
    (c) Document your interactions with employees.
    (d) Reduce the amount of direct supervision of your employees.

19. Which of the following is true of the relationship between stress and productivity? [p.158]
    (a) Stress lowers productivity.
    (b) Productivity lowers stress.
    (c) Some stress is necessary to be productive. ✓
    (d) Most stress is harmful and causes work-related problems.

20. When supervising a diverse workforce it is important that you: [p.165]
    (a) get direction from your boss on how to supervise.
    (b) ignore individual differences of opinion.
    (c) hire an equal number of males and females.
    (d) let people know where you stand on diversity. ✓

21. The motivation factor that ranks highest for most employees is: [p.140]
    (a) interesting work.
    (b) good pay.
    (c) recognition for a job well done. ✓
    (d) tactful discipline.

22. The primary benefit of teamwork is that: [p.134]
    (a) the manager does not have to work so hard.
    (b) people working together can accomplish more than individuals. ✓
    (c) a team creates competition which increases productivity.
    (d) everyone enjoys being part of a team.

23. As a first-line supervisor, your time will be divided between working and supervising. Approximately how much of your time should you expect to spend supervising others? [p.4]
    (a) 0–15 percent
    (b) 16–35 percent ✓
    (c) 36–55 percent
    (d) 56–75 percent

P.46 24. Communication is most successful when:
(a) the sender delivers a powerful message.
(b) the receiver tries to listen effectively.
(c) the sender achieves specific results.
(d) the message is presented visually.

P.116 25. When taking disciplinary action you should:
(a) always start by suspending the employee.
(b) be glad that you have to take action.
(c) involve as many employees as possible.
(d) focus on the employee's behavior.

Index

Accepting responsibility for actions, 27
Accessibility, 26
Active listening, 54–55, 132. *See also* Listening
Age Discrimination in Employment Act, 163
Agenda, 57–58, 66
 reviewing the, 58
Americans with Disabilities Act (ADA), 163
Attitude, 3, 6–7

Behavior, 12
 discussing behavior issues, 116
Being a supervisor and a technical expert, 9
"Big boss", 1, 29
Body language, 54, 58
Brainstorming session, 59–60
 rules for conducting, 60
Building a team, 38, 40, 123. *See also* Team development
 challenge of, 123
Building respect, 22

Cadwell, Charles M., 105–106
Cellular technology, 66
Civil Rights Act, 163
Coaching, 91, 95
 the process, 91
 when to quit, 95
Coaching employees, 71–72, 88
 vs. orientation and training, 88
Coaching situation, 88
 key factors in assessing a, 88
Coaching worksheet, 92–94
Common priorities, 31
Commons, Michael L., 73. *See also* Stevens-Long, Judith

Communicating, 38–39
 levels of, 39
Communicating anticipated problems or roadblocks, 33
Communicate expectations, 127, 142
Communication, 45–47
 breakdown in, 46, 47. *See also* Communication problems
 definition of, 46
 four part, 45
 process, 45
 successful, 47
 taking responsibility for, 47
Communication breakdowns, 47
 examples, 47, 49
Communication problems, 46
Communication process, 46
Communication skills, 45–46
 and productivity, 45
Communication technology, 45, 63, 67
Computer systems, 66–67
Conferencing, 65
Confidence level, 2
 rating, 2, 180
Confidence level revaluation, 180
Confidential information, 64, 66
Confidentiality, 66. *See also* Confidential information
Conflict management styles, 111–112. *See also* Workplace conflict
 types of, 112
Constructive discharge, 162
Continuous improvement, 29
Corrective feedback, 99, 103–104
 focus of, 103
 worksheet for, 104

Crediting others, 132. *See also* Teamwork, Sharing glory
Customers, 8
 interactions with, 8

Daily list, 155
 prioritizing the, 155
Daily time log, 156–157
Davis, Jeffrey H., 88, 95
Day-to-day actions. *See* Day-to-day activities
Day-to-day activities, 22, 23
 monitoring, 23
Day-to-day operations, 7–8
 responsibility for, 7
Delegation, 128, 139, 145, 147–148
 follow up, 148
 guidelines for successful, 145
 importance of, 145
 preparation for, 148–149
 selecting an individual for, 147
 supporting the person, 148
Delegation checklist, 145–146
Delegation skill, 16
Department of Labor, 162
Determining priorities, 151
Developing people, 38–39
 orientation, training and coaching, 39
Development activities
 types of, 72
Difficult behaviors, 107–108
 causes of, 107
 strategies for dealing with, 107, 110
 types of, 107
Disciplinary action, 40, 99, 116, 118–119
 methods for taking, 99, 116, 119

Disciplinary action (continued)
    organizational policies and
        procedures, 118–120
Disciplinary options
    oral warning, 117
    suspension, 117–118
    termination, 117–118
    written warning, 117
Discipline, 116
    negative connotation, 116
Distance management, 161,
        168–169. *See also* Virtual
        work
    uses of, 169
    what, why, and when of, 168
Distance manager, 41, 168–169
    being successful as a, 169–170
Diverse workforce, 165
    supervising a, 165
Diversity, 165–166
    analyzing, 166
    developing for, 166
    in an organization, 166
    role in supervising, 165
Diversity awareness, 167
Dos and don'ts, 34–35

*E*ffective communication
        techniques, 46
Effective first-line supervisors, 21,
        26, 29
    personal qualities of, 21, 26
Effective supervision, 21
    key competencies for, 21
Effective written communication,
        45
    guidelines for, 45
Electronic communication, 63
    guidelines for using, 63
Electronic messaging
    e-mail, 63
    instant messaging, 63
    text messaging, 63
Emotional reactions, 53
Employee rights, 162
Employee training, 78
    plan for, 71
Employees, Employees, 7, 14, 21,
        23, 28, 50, 53, 89, 100, 102,
        139, 144
    coachability factor, 89
    conflicts between, 23
    experienced, 14
    first line of contact for, 7
    "friendly competition"
        among, 100
    having belief in, 28
    holding the attention of, 50
    impression of, 7
    new, 14

obtaining top performance from,
        139, 144
    positive example for, 22
    recognizing and rewarding,
        102
    responses from, 53
Evaluation and goal setting process,
        184
Exchange of ideas, 52
Experience, 22

*F*ace-to-face communication, 63
Fair Labor Standards Act, 163
Family and Medical Leave Act
        (FMLA), 163
Feedback, 28, 33
Feedback systems, 100–101
First-line supervisor, 1–3, 5–9,
        22, 78, 91, 99, 129, 134, 139,
        141, 143–144, 154, 161–162,
        173, 179, 182. *See also*
        Supervisor
    addressing the paradoxes of, 11
    being effective as a, 143
    coaching role, 91
    creating the right environment as
        a, 134
    demands on, 5
    differences between employees
        and, 3
    ensuring success as a, 180
    flexiblility as a, 154
    leading by example, 144
    legal issues for, 161–162
    paradoxes encountered by, 1, 9
    positive impact as a, 8
    promotion to, 1
    "recipes for success" as a, 139
    requirements for being
        successful, 1, 6
    responsibilities of, 7
    role and responsibilities in
        implementing change, 173
    role in motivation, 141
    transition from employee to,
        179
    transition from team member
        to, 1
    using an effective, 22
Focus, 6
Follow-Up. *See* Training, Four-step
        method
Fortune 1000 companies, 168
Four-step method, 78–79
Four-step training planner, 78
    follow-up, 80, 83
    preparation, 80, 81
    presentation and demonstration,
        80, 81, 83
    tryout, 80, 83

*G*allup organization, 141
Getting the work done, 38, 41
Good work habits, 33
Gossip and rumors, 34
Government laws, 162
Grapevine gossip, 57
Grievance policy, 35

*H*arvard Business School, 150
Human resources department,
        163–164

"*I*" messages, 108
Immigration and Nationality Act,
        163
Importance of first-line supervisors,
        18
Individual benefits, 124
Information, 5, 47
Information available, 15
    and leadership style, 15
Information motivation, 6
Interdepartmental cooperation,
        17
Internet, 65. *See also* Intranet
Intranet, 65

*J*ob knowledge, 22
Job motivation factors,
        140–141

*K*ey competencies, 38, 41
    strengths, weaknesses, and
        opportunities, 41
Kilmann, Ralph H., 113

*L*eadership style, 12–15
    balanced, 14
    choice of. *See* Selection of
        leadership style
    extremes, 14–15
    goals of, 15
    people-oriented, 12, 14
    scoring, 14
    selection of, 15
    task-oriented, 12, 14
Leadership style considerations,
        16–17
Legal action, 163
Legal issues, 41, 164
Listener needs, 51
Listening, 50, 54
    problems and solutions, 50
    without interrupting, 54
Listening habits, 52
    steps to improve, 52–54
Listening skills, 45, 52
    factors for improving, 45

*M*aintaining focus, 72

Making commitments, 132
Management and leadership
    skills, 10
Managing change, 161, 173–175.
    See also Stages of change
    as a first-line spervisor, 174
    role of the first-line supervisor
        in, 174
Managing people, 23, 38, 40
Managing workplace conflict, 40
Marx, Groucho, 60
MBWA (management by walking
    around) 91
Meeting evaluation tool, 59
Meeting planning checklist, 58
Meetings, 45, 56, 57, 58
    closing, 58
    conducting, 58
    planning and conducting, 45, 56,
        58
    preparation, 57
Middle management, 8
Milestone chart, 152
Motivation, 5
    and behavior, 142

Negative behaviors. See Difficult
    behaviors, 73
New employee orientation, 71, 73,
    76, 78
    conducting, 77
    goal of, 73
    process of, 77, 78
Non-monetary rewards, 102
Number of priorities, 4, 6

Ongoing professional development,
    184
open door policy See also
    Accessibility, 26
Open-ended questions, 54, 83, 114
Opportunity to perform, 87
Organization, 1, 2, 4, 8, 17, 18, 32
    flattening, 8
    power centers within, 17
    priorities for the, 32
Organization ladder, 4
Organization of work, 10
Organization policies, 162
Organization talent, 7, 8
    development of, 7, 8
Organizational constraints, 16
Orientation checklist, 75, 76
Orientation program See also
    New employee orientation, 73
    objectives of, 73–75
Overcontrol, 146

"Parking lot" technique, 58
Partners, 31

expectations between, 31
Partnership development, 31
Partnerships, 31
Paying attention, 50
Payne, Vivette, 175
People development, 71, 72
    benefits of, 72
    importance of, 72
    steps involved in, 71
People management, 99
People skills, 10
Performance appraisal process, 105,
    106
    purposes and benefits of the, 105
Performance appraisal, 40
Performance feedback, 40, 99–101
    providing, 101
Performance management tool, 103
Performance motivation,
    139–140
    factors affecting. See also
        motivation factors
Performance problems and
    issues, 23
Personal action plan, 179, 181, 183
    being realistic about, 183
Personal qualities, 29
Personal responsibility, 28
Personal standards, 144
    setting, 26
Planning and managing change, 175
Planning and organization, 149, 150
    imperatives of, 150
Planning cycle, 153
    asking the right questions, 153
Positive feedback, 100, 101, 143
Positive relationship, 35
    developing and maintaining, 35
Post-training meeting, 86
Power centers and formal structure,
    16–17
Preparing an agenda, 57
Presentation/demonstration. See
    Training, Four-step method,
    52
Presenting ideas, 51
Pre-training meeting, 86
Pirorities
    multiple, 3
    specific, 3
Projects, 32
    information on the progress
        of, 32

Quality and service, 27

Receiver, 47
Recording decisions, 58
Reinemund, Steven, 71, 165
Relationship potential, 30, 33

maximizing the, 33
Resolving workplace conflict. See
    Workplace conflict,
    successfully managing, 164
Role model, 165

Safety, 162
Selection of leadership style, 14
Self-assessment, 2, 3, 11
    issues in, 3
    using the results of, 11
Sender, 47
Sense of humor, 85, 133
Setting goals, 72
Setting priorities, 28
Sharing resources, 133
Shift of focus. See also Focus, 2
Situational leadership, 1
Skill areas, 182
    rating skill levels, 181, 183
Span of control, 7, 8
Speaker, 52
Specific results, 47
Stages of change, 173, 174
Stephen Covey, 156
Stevens–Long, Judith. See also
    Commons, Michael L. 73
Stress, 139, 157, 158
    effect on productivity, 139, 157
Success, 27
    believability of, 27
    inspiring, 27
Successful plan, 150
Supervising in a changing
    environment, 38
Supervising tasks and learning
    skills, 11
Supervision, 139
Supervisor, 1, 21, 72, 127 See also
    First-line supervisor
    being effective as a, 127
    role of the, 21
    rules to follow as a, 10
Supervisory roles, 22–23
    handling problems and
        issues, 22
    providing resources, 22
Supervisory skills, 18
Supervisory success, 38
Supportive environment, 87

Task force See also Team, 130
Task vs. people, 12
Team, 2, 5, 7, 123, 125, 127
    definition of, 125, 127
    subdividing a, 125
    transform a group into a, 123, 127
Team builder, 3
Team development, 41, 123,
    134–135

Team development (continued)
  obstacles to, 123, 134
  removing obstacles to, 135
Team member, 3, 28, 126–127, 130
  being valuable as a. *See* valuable team member, 123
  common approach, 126
  complementary skills, 126
  mutual accountability, 127
  purpose and goals, 126
Team spirit, 125
Teamwork, 123–124, 127–129, 143
  benefits of, 124, 125
  improving, 129
  share expectations, 127
  sharing glory, 129
  sharing responsibilities, 128
  value of, 124
Technical skills, 4
The 7 Habits of Highly Effective People, 156
The, 80/20 rule, 143
The boss, 1, 29, 34 *See also* "Big boss"
  complaining about, 34
  positive working relationship with, 30
  responsibilities, 1
  working with, 29
Things to avoid, 34, 35
Thomas, Kenneth W. 113
Thomas–Kilmann Conflict Mode Instrument, 113
Time allocation, 4
Time available, 15
  and leadership style, 15
Time commitment, 5, 6
Time management, 139, 155, 156
  effect on productivity, 139

The management systems, 155
  Day runner, 155
  Day timer, 155
  Franklin Covey, 155
Time saving, 56
Timetable, 151
Top performance, 142
Trainer, 83–85
  being effective as a, 83
  rating one's qualities as a, 85
  skills necessary to be effective, 84, 85
Training, 10, 78, 81–83, 86. *See also* Employee training
  benefits of, 78
  four-step method, 84
  making sure it is effective, 86
Tryout. *See* Training, Four-step method

Undercontrol, 146
Untrained employees, 79
Upper management, 7, 28, 41, 99, 124
  demands from, 28
Upward communication, 30, 32, 33
  establishing guidelines for, 32

Valuable team member, 131
  keys to Being a, 131
Virtual employees, 41
Virtual offices, 41

Virtual work, 161, 168–169, 171–172. *See also* Distance management
  dos and don'ts for implementing, 171
  organization success factors, 171

Virtual worker, 170, 171
  being successful as a, 170
  considerations when selecting a, 171
Vision, mission, and goals, 32
Voice mail, 64

WII-FM (what's in it for me) 51, 61
Work, 22, 139
  organization and planning, 22
  procedures for planning and organizing, 139
Work environment, 161
  changes in the, 161
Work group, 12
Work plan, 154
  developing a, 154
Workforce, 2000 study, 164
Working together, 123
  importance of, 123
Working with difficult employees, 99, 106
  strategies for, 99
Workplace, 31
  written documents in the, 31
  federal legislation in the, 163
Workplace conflict, 99, 110, 113, 115
  causes of, 99, 110
management of, 99, 110–111
  successfully managing, 113
Workplace issues, 133. *See also* Workplace conflict
Written communication, 60–62
  evaluating, 62
  organizing, 61
  reports and memos, 60